CONVERSATIONS ON IRVING STREET

JOSIAH ROYCE'S CONTRIBUTION TO SYMBOLIC INTERACTIONISM

by

Darrick Lee Brake
West Liberty University

Edited by

Corey Reiner
and
Frank Tridico

Series in Sociology

VERNON PRESS

www.vernonpress.com

In the Americas:
Vernon Press
1000 N West Street,
Suite 1200, Wilmington,
Delaware 19801
United States

In the rest of the world:
Vernon Press
C/Sancti Espiritu 17,
Malaga, 29006
Spain

Series in Sociology

Library of Congress Control Number: 2019940483

ISBN: 978-1-62273-848-9

Also available:

978-1-62273-505-1 [Hardback]; 978-1-62273-757-4 [PDF, E-Book]

Cover design by Vernon Press.
Cover image: Josiah Royce (1855-1916), The Royce Society.

This book is dedicated to my Father (who I think about everyday),
my Mother (who always makes me laugh),
my sister (whoshares my love for the social sciences),
and Kayla, who has supported me every step of the way.

.

ACKNOWLEDGEMENTS

I wish to thank the following individuals: Dr. Larry Tifft, Dr. Gil Musolf, and Dr. Blaine Stevenson. Without the combined effort of these three amazing individuals, this book would have never been possible. Their dedication and assistance throughout the creation of this monograph exemplifies a level of mentorship that many, including myself, strive for each and every day. The culmination of their constant work and thoughtful effort not only made this book better, but also made me a better person. For that I can never give thanks enough.

I would also like to extend a special thanks to Dr. Gil Musolf for being a mentor and taking me under his theoretical wing. The knowledge gained from our conversations yielded more than just new insight into theory; it helped me become a better sociologist and an even greater person. I also feel the need to thank Dr. Bernard Meltzer, whose knowledge and shared ideas of the theoretical world will stay with me forever. I want to give thanks to Dr. Bill Tregea who started me on this theoretical wave that I continue to ride. My only hope is that someday I will be able to impact at least one student the way Bill has impacted me.

I also want to give a special thanks to Dr. Larry Reynolds whose ideas, suggestions, and comments on this book not only improved it, but also improved me as well. It improved me as a writer, an academic, and a thinker. My only hope is that someday I will have such a profound impact on at least one student.

ABSTRACT

The focus of this monograph is the contribution of Josiah Royce's academic work (1913-1917) to the development of classical symbolic interactionist thought. This research centers on critically evaluating the works of Royce and assessing how his ideas and social philosophy were significant contributions to both symbolic interactionist thought and sociological theory. An effort is also made to understand the philosophical influences that shaped Royce's social and philosophical thought. The data for this project came from library resources ranging from books and articles to numerous archives.

The major concepts of George Herbert Mead (*Mind, Self, and Society*) and Herbert Blumer's core synthesized components of classical symbolic interactionist thought (*Symbolic Interactionism: Perspective and Method*) are compared and contrasted with Royce's social philosophy.

The results of this research demonstrate that Royce's later academic works (1913-1917) closely resemble the basic ideas of Mead. Royce's constructs of the theory of signs, interpretation, the doctrine of signs, and the mind closely correspond to Mead's concepts of language and meaning, defining meaning, the generalized other, and the mind. There is also a strong correspondence between Royce's concepts and Blumer's synthesis of the three basic premises and eight root images that outline the theoretical core of symbolic interactionist thought.

In sum, this research provides a holistic approach to Royce's academic work and the social philosophy that shaped symbolic interactionist theory. It also provides a historical sketch that places his contributions into their proper socio-historical time frame and investigates the development of his ideas. This monograph thoroughly explores the sociological constructs of an American philosopher whose contributions to the development of symbolic interactionism has been largely unnoticed.

TABLE OF CONTENTS

FOREWORD

Let us assume that David R. Maines (2001: 8) is correct in considering a theoretical perspective "… as an array of concepts and ontological claims that prefigure inquiry and analysis." Employing such a definition, one can probably agree with James F. Short, Jr.'s assertion that the theoretical framework Herbert Blumer dubbed *symbolic interactionism* is one of the "… three most important theoretical perspectives in sociology" (1980: xi). One may even find oneself in general accord with both Don Martindale's statement that "… symbolic interactionism has had an influence upon almost every contemporary sociologist" (1981: 347) and with Maines' bold assertion that "… the entire field of sociology, without being aware of it, has been moving in the direction of symbolic interactionism" (2001:2).

Few would deny Manis and Meltzer's (1978: 440) claim that symbolic interactionism is the most sociological of all the social psychologies. Fewer still would deny that interactionism has been, and indeed remains, a most important theoretical perspective within American sociology and that both its audience and practitioners increasingly come from a growing number of nations.

This book by young scholar Darrick Brake wishes to make a contribution to interactionism by broadening our understanding of its intellectual origins. Brake's master's degree, upon which this book is based, was written at Central Michigan University, an institution whose sociology department has long been a real stronghold of symbolic interactionism. Brake has been exposed to the thought and research of several scholars long concerned with enhancing their understanding of the social, intellectual, and philosophical underpinnings of their own theoretical framework. He seeks to become a part of this larger effort at self-understanding by focusing on an intellectual forerunner of symbolic interactionism whose writings have received insufficient attention.

A number of symbolic interactionists have pointed to the perspective's philosophical/intellectual antecedents. After all these years, the list provided by Manis and Meltzer remains perhaps the best available: (1) evolutionism, (2) German idealism, (3) the Scottish moralists, (4) pragmatism, and (5) functional psychology (1978: 1-3). It is the fourth listed of these antecedents, pragmatism, that captures Darrick Brake's attention.

Pragmatic philosophers who are said to have influenced symbolic interactionism are Josiah Royce (see Joas, 1993; Cook, 1993), Charles S. Pierce, William James, John Dewey, George Herbert Mead, J. A. Tufts, Ella Flagg Young, Edward Scribner Ames, James Rowland Angell, and Addison Weber Moore (Reynolds, 1987: 17; Reynolds, 2003: 46; Deegan,2001: xxv). The last six of these philosophers were all members of the dominant Chicago school of pragmatism. James was on the faculty at Harvard University for a lengthy time, and Royce taught there for thirty-four years. Mead interacted with James frequently and Royce was his teacher (Aboulafia, 2012: 2). Pierce, on the other hand, was excluded "… from the circle of academic philosophy" (Boskoff, 1969: 325). He exerted much of his early influence on the scientifically inclined members of the Hyperion Club (Mills, 1966).

Outside of the Chicago school of pragmatism, only James's influence on the general interactionist framework has been highly significant and of long standing. Pierce's impact has been recognized only belatedly, and apart from direct positive influence on Mead, his greatest influence is not on interactionism in general but on that variety of symbolic interactionism known as the Iowa School (Reynolds 2003: 47-48).

Josiah Royce seems to have been pretty much left out of the picture. As a sociologist of knowledge, I wonder why! Why would one of the four key founders of pragmatism as a philosophical movement (Manis and Meltzer, 1978: 7; Reynolds, 2003: 46) be ignored? Why would so many, though by no means all, contemporary interactionists either fail to cite his work (Denzin, 1992: Maines, 2001; Meltzer, Petras, and Reynolds, 1975; Musolf, 1998; Prus, 1996), mention him only in passing (Manis and Meltzer, 1978; Stryker, 1980), or offer only strictly limited commentary (Deegan, 2001; Reynolds, 2003) on "the single most important idealist in the United States" (Martindale, 1981: 266)?

These, however, are not Darrick Brake's questions. They are not his concern. Rather, he simply wants of demonstrate: (1) that Royce's writings have something to offer today's interactionists; (2) that Royce's views on many topics are compatible with those of such intellectual powerhouses as his student George Herbert Mead and those of interactionism's once titular head, the late Herbert Blumer; and (3) that Royce should be fully accepted as one of symbolic interactionism's legitimate forerunners, even if, in the long run, his influence remains less than that of Mead, Dewey, James, or even Pierce. Brake attempts to accomplish all this by first placing Royce's work in its philosophical-historical context and then showing the compatibility between such Roycean intellectual formations as the "Doctrine of Signs" and the "Theory of Signs, Symbols, and Interpretations" and then-developing patterns of symbolic interactionist thought.

In my opinion, Brake has gone a long way toward making his case that Royce's ideas should engage our attention. This short book, Brake's first, merits a read.

Larry T. Reynolds
Emeritus Professor of Sociology
Central Michigan University

References cited

Aboulafia, Mitchell, 2012. "George Herbert Mead." *Stanford Encyclopedia of Philosophy*. plato.stanford.edu/entries/mead: 1-13.

Boskoff, Alvin, 1969. *Theory in American Sociology: Major Sources and Applications*. New York: Thomas Y Crowell.

Cook, Gary A., 1993. *Georg Herbert Mead: The Making of a Ssocial Pragmatist*. Urbana: University of Illinois Press.

Deegan, Mary Jo, 2001. "Introduction: George Herbert Mead's First Book." In George H. Mead, *Essays in Social Psychology*. New Brunswick: Transaction Publishers, xi-xliv.

Denzin, Norman K., 1992. *Symbolic Interactionism and Cultural Studies: The Politics of Interpretation*. Oxford: Blackwell.

Joas, Hans, 1993. *Pragmatism and Social Theory*. Chicago: University of Chicago Press.

Maines, David R., 2001. *The Faultline of Consciousness: A View of Interactionism in Sociology*. New York: Aldine De Gruyter.

Manis, Jerome G., and Bernard N. Meltzer, eds., 1978. *Symbolic Interaction: A Reader in Social Psychology*. Boston: Allyn and Bacon.

Martindale, Don, 1981. *The Nature and Types of Sociological Theory*. Boston: Houghton Mifflin Co.

Meltzer, Bernard N., John W. Petras, and Larry T. Reynolds, 1975. *Symbolic Interactionism: Genesis, Varieties, and Criticism*. London: Routledge and Kegan Paul.

Mills, C. Wright, 1966. *Sociology and Pragmatism: The Higher Learning in America*. New York: Galaxy Books.

Musolf, Gil Richard, 1998. *Structure and Agency in Everyday Life: An Introduction to Social Psychology*. Dix Hills, NY: General Hall, Inc.

Prus, Robert, 1996. *Symbolic Interaction and Ethnographic Research: Intersubjectivity and the Study of Human Lived Experience*. Albany: State University of New York Press.

Reynolds, Larry T., 1987. *Interactionism: Exposition and Critique*. Dix Hills, NY: General Hall, Inc.

Reynolds, Larry T., 2003. "Intellectual Antecedents." In Larry T. Reynolds
   and Nancy Herman-Kinney, eds., *Handbook of Symbolic Interactionism.*
   Walnut Creek, CA: Altamira Press: 39-58.

Short, James F., Jr., 1980. "Foreword." In Sheldon Stryker, *Symbolic
   Interactionism: A Social Structural Version.* Menlo Park, CA:
   Benjamin/Cummings Publishing Company: xi.

INTRODUCTION

The research presented in this monograph began several years ago when I was working on my master's thesis at Central Michigan University. Through several conversations with Dr. Bernie Meltzer, I became aware of the academic works of Josiah Royce who I had, at the time, very little knowledge about. After I began reading his works and investigating his basic ideas and concepts I wanted to know more about Royce and decided to focus my entire master's thesis on the subject of Josiah Royce and his academic works.

Once I began investigating Royce's social philosophy, I noticed that his ideas had interlinkages and connections to the basic tenets and concepts of early symbolic interactionism. These connections lead me to ask the research question: Did Josiah Royce and his ideas on social philosophy make a contribution to early symbolic interactionist theory? In order for me to answer this question, I would have to become more familiar with his work, his ideas, and basic concepts. This is what I set out to do with my master's thesis.

This monograph represents a culmination of the research I performed for my master's thesis and additional research in the topic of Josiah Royce's contribution to symbolic interactionism. The major focus of this book will be centered on critically evaluating the works of Josiah Royce and discuss how his ideas and social philosophy made contributions to symbolic interactionist thought and sociological theory. The data for my research came from a range of different library resources ranging from books and articles, to the use of numerous archives. The primary work for the majority of this book will be that of reading, interpreting, and analyzing Josiah Royce's major academic works that illustrate his connections to early symbolic interactionist thought.

There are two major tasks that require an explanation in order to assess the contributions made by Josiah Royce to the development of symbolic interactionism. The first major task, as discussed in chapter one, is to place Royce and his ideas into the proper historical-philosophical time period. By doing this, I hope to establish that (1) the academic works of

Royce did *not* predate the early formative years of the philosophy of pragmatism (one of the major vein of thoughts that developed symbolic interactionism), (2) that Royce created and published academic works at the *same time* as the other early American pragmatists, meaning that he did *not* miss the crucial developmental years, and (3) that considering the time in which Royce wrote and lived, in comparison with William James, John Dewey, and Charles Sanders Peirce, he did *not* postdate the development of pragmatic thought and symbolic interactionist theory.

The second major task is to substantively assess Royce's "Theory of signs, symbols, and interpretations" and the "Doctrine of signs" and to explore as many connections as possible to the development of symbolic interactionist thought. Royce's book *The Problem of Christianity* (1913) and the article "Mind" (1917) are his most critical works in discussing the connections between symbolic interactionism and his own ideas. There is a summary of Royce's basic ideas from *The Problem of Christianity* in chapters two through four. Chapter two looks at his theory of perception, conception, and interpretation. Chapter three focuses on his discussion of the will to interpret which layouts his ideas on the interpretive process and chapter four summarizes in detail Royce's concept of the doctrine of signs. There is a detailed discussion and summary of the ideas presented in Royce's article titled *Mind* in chapter five. This article represents his late and final work on the topic of perception, conception, and interpretation.

To explore and define symbolic interactionism and its meaning for this research, the basic tenets and ideas of George Herbert Mead (chapter six) as presented in his book *Mind, Self, and Society* (1934) and those of Herbert Blumer (chapter eight) in his book *Symbolic Interactionism: Perspective and Method* (1969), are utilized by focusing on Mead's and Blumer's works a wide net can be cast in terms of comparing and contrasting their ideas on symbolic interactionism with those of Royce. This comparison allows an investigation of the connections between Royce's basic ideas and both Mead's classical symbolic interactionism and Blumer's more recent developments of symbolic interactionism. These connections and interlinkages are discussed in chapter seven (Royce and Mead) and in chapter eight (Royce and Blumer).

The final chapter (chapter 10) summarizes and discusses all the interlinkages between Josiah Royce and George Herbert Mead, and Royce and Herbert Blumer. The final section of this chapter will discuss how the connections between these individuals' works suggest that Josiah Royce has definitely made a contribution to symbolic interactionist thought and theory. This contribution suggests that Royce is just as important as other Pragmatists when his ideas are laid out and discussed in relation to symbolic interactionism. As well as suggesting that Royce should be viewed as a contributor to early symbolic interactionism in the same manner as James, Dewey, and Peirce. By focusing this research on placing Royce's work into the proper socio-historical time period and through exploring his philosophical works, my overall goal for this research is to provide insight into the works and life of an American philosopher whose work (and contribution to symbolic interactionism) "has been misunderstood and misjudged" (Stuhr 1987, 179).

CHAPTER I

PLACING ROYCE INTO EARLY PRAGMATIC HISTORY

In order to place Royce's work within the proper socio-philosophical context and within the time he wrote, two tasks must be undertaken. These are (1) establishing the dates and times within which Royce produced academic works pertinent to his career and its development, and (2) placing Royce's academic work within the larger context of the writings of James, Dewey, and Peirce. Royce wrote and produced his relevant academic works and his social philosophy during the formative years of American pragmatism. The establishment of this overall point will assist in linking Royce to symbolic interactionism.

Royce began his academic career at Harvard University in the fall semester of 1882. During his first three years at Harvard, Royce was surrounded by academic powerhouses and published very little, though he attended seminars, gave speeches, and wrote lectures for the courses he taught. This academic drought would end in 1885 when Royce published his first major work, *The Religious Aspect of Philosophy* (1885). The theme of this work centered on the idea that religion (theology) and philosophy can be related to one another by comparing and contrasting each discipline's major ideas.

At this time, the other major pragmatists: James, Dewey, and Peirce, who started their careers much earlier, were making strides and producing major works. In 1885, psychologist and pragmatist James produced an article titled, "On the Function of Cognition" (1885), while Charles Sanders Peirce produced one of his major works, "On the Algebra of Logic" (1885).

1886 through 1892

Royce's next major academic work, *California: A Study of American Character* (1886), represents a change in focus. On the surface, the book is just that: A history of the state of California, though it could be considered a historical ethnography. It represents a brief history of California's development as a state, and it chronicles the daily lives of early Californians and their struggles in the frontier west. These struggles ranged from land and mining disputes to crime, prostitution, and the issues of frontier racism. As an early work, it hints at the beginnings of Royce's concerns about the dissolving communities out West.

During the time period of 1886–1892, numerous academic contributions were published by other American pragmatists. Dewey published two major articles: "The Psychological Standpoint" (1886) and "Psychology as Philosophic Method" (1886). The year 1886 is significant because it marks Peirce's "visit to Cambridge, where he delivered lectures on his cosmological system to William James, Josiah Royce, John Fiske, and others" (Brent 1998, 369). A year later, Peirce wrote *A Guess at the Riddle* and Dewey published *Psychology* (1887). In 1888, Dewey published *The Ethics of Democracy* and in 1889, Peirce published scientific and philosophic definitions in the *Century Dictionary*. Also, in 1889, James published the article, "The Psychology of Belief" and later in 1890, the major academic work titled *Principles of Psychology*. The end of this six-year time period leads us to Royce's third major publication, which reflects a return to his traditional roots in philosophy.

In 1892, Royce published the book titled *The Spirit of Modern Philosophy*. It represents an overview of the philosophers who had impacted Royce's thinking. It included a chapter-by-chapter analysis of the philosophies of such greats like Baruch Spinoza, Immanuel Kant, Johann Gottlieb Fichte, Georg Wilhelm Friedrich Hegel, and Arthur Schopenhauer. Each philosopher and the ideas that they developed are put into chronological historical order. What separates this piece from others similar to it is the difference in format. Instead of this book becoming a tirade on the problems of western philosophy, Royce focused his attention on what each individual philosopher had to offer in terms of ideas. Royce, in forming his own philosophical ideas, took the best social thoughts of these different thinkers and created a hybrid theory. Essentially, Royce took the best from each person and abandoned what he believed were their weaknesses.

1892 through 1898

From the years 1892–1898, there was a marked increase in the production of academic work from the American pragmatists. Dewey published the major academic work: *Introduction to Philosophy* (1892). Then, in 1894, he published the book, *Study of Ethics* and the article "Social Psychology".

Dewey published his next book, *Interest as Related to the Will*, in 1896. *The Significance of The Problem of Knowledge* was published in 1897. The year 1897 became significant for James, as he published one of his most well-known academic works, *The Will to Believe*.

After publication of his *The Spirit of Modern Philosophy* (1892), Royce did not produce a major publication for six years. At the end of this downtime, in 1898, he published his fourth major academic work, *Studies of Good and Evil*, which represents an academic work that is focused on the philosophical issue of theodicy. He pulled biblical and theological references from numerous religious perspectives and then applied philosophical concepts and ideas to make statements about the nature of good and evil. This method of explaining theological problems through philosophical means is original. Royce was not trying to prove theology or philosophy wrong. Instead, he was attempting to synthesize both academic areas.

1899 through 1908

Royce's fifth academic work, the two-volume *The World and The Individual* (1901), is a collection of essays that summarize his own ideas on metaphysics and present his concept called the fourth conception of being. In this work, Royce refutes the three major teleological views of reality: to be is to be independent, to be is to be immediate, and to be is to be valid. In their place, he presents a fourth conception: the idea that being creates meaning and therefore furnishes the goal of purpose. This book presents many of Royce's major concepts and philosophical principles. It not only explores his unique metaphysical position, but it also doubles as an example of using modern logic to solve real philosophical problems.

Like Royce, in this time period (1899–1901), the other American pragmatists continued to write and publish. Dewey, in 1899, published the book, *Psychology and The Philosophic Method*, and in 1900 produced the article, "Psychology and Social Practice". Later that same year, Dewey reviewed Royce's book, *The World and The Individual*, and in 1901, Dewey published *Dictionary of Philosophy and Psychology*. At this same time, in 1901, James worked on the famed Gifford lectures. The next year, 1902, James published another one of his most famous works: *The Varieties of Religious Experience* (1901), and during this time, Peirce became a contributor to James Mark Baldwin's book, the *Dictionary of Philosophy and Psychology*. Royce did not produce another major work until 1904, when he published *Outlines of Psychology*.

This major academic work, Royce's sixth, shows his versatility by writing on subjects outside the realm of theology and strict philosophy. This book outlines Royce's basic ideas and his perspective on the discipline of psychology. The majority of the ideas contained within focus on the individual, and more specifically on how an individual develops. One chapter is dedicated to the human self and the social being. It provides insight into the social development of humans. From this academic work, an argument can be made that Royce was a social philosopher.

The seventh academic work published by Royce is titled *The Philosophy of Loyalty* (1908), which can be summarized as a metaphysical investigation into three areas: defining what loyalty is, what constitutes being loyal to one another, and the question of whether anyone can be loyal. To answer these questions, Royce looks at loyalty from both a theological perspective and a philosophical perspective—the same method that he used in his fourth major publication. His synthesized approach allows him to cover more ground on the subject of loyalty. It also allows him to deflect criticism because of a lack of perspective, (i.e., he did not approach the topic solely on the basis of theology or solely on the basis of philosophy). Overall, Royce's study on the subject of loyalty led him to believe that there is a potential connection between the philosophical conception of loyalty and the religious conception of loyalty. Thus, to be properly investigated, loyalty in and of itself requires a synthesis of theology and philosophy.

1908 through 1912

For the American pragmatists, the time period 1909–1912 was a productive set of years. In the year 1908, Dewey published the article "What Does Pragmatism Mean by Practical.". The following year, in 1909, James prepared to create and deliver his famed Hibbert lectures. Later that same year, James published the article "A Pluralistic Universe". The following year, in 1910, James died at Chocorua, New Hampshire on August 26th. The death of James was only the first of many tragedies for the other pragmatists. Royce did not publish another major work for two years after his long-time friend and colleague died.

His next publication, his eighth, came in 1912. Titled *The Sources of Religious Insight*, this book marks a movement by Royce to focus on a more theological subject. Here, Royce examined and scrutinized different types of religious beliefs and ideas. As a whole, Royce was not impressed by many of the modern conceptions of religion and belief systems, so he set out to explain his own brand of religious ideology called the "religion of loyalty." The "religion of loyalty" is distinctively different from other religious concepts on two bases: First, Royce does not accept the idea that religions are based in pure individualism, and second, that "church" is more of a social experience shared amongst members, as opposed to an individual experience.

Within twelve months of the publications of *The Sources of Religious Insight* (1912), Royce published his ninth major academic work, *The Problem of Christianity* (1913). It sought to answer the question of whether a modern man can be a Christian. To answer this question, one must strip Christianity down to its bare essentials and remove the myths, stories, and falsehoods associated with it. This stripping away process meant de-emphasizing the stories of Jesus before, during, and after his life and cutting away the inspirational stories. When Royce performed this peeling away process, he discovered that the Christian faith has, at its core, a set of universal ideas that speaks volumes about our reality and the world around us. These ideas involved the following concepts: interpretation, comparison, signs, meaning, and the formation of a community of interpretation. These core concepts are of particular interest to this book because of their links to symbolic interactionism.

1912 through 1916

The final time period, 1912–1916, held great promise but presented great tragedy for the philosophy known as pragmatism. In 1912, Dewey wrote the article, "Reply to Professor Royce's Critique of Instrumentalism." This was not his last article; (he lived well into the 1950s), but for the purposes of this book, I am going to stop with this 1912 article because Dewey outlived the other pragmatists and published well beyond the early twentieth century. The year 1913 proved to be interesting because Peirce was able to listen to Royce's four lectures on the 'doctrine of signs'. A year after Royce's lectures, on April 19, 1914, Peirce died of cancer at Arisbe, his estate in Pennsylvania.

After Peirce's death, Royce would not publish his tenth work for another two years. Royce's tenth major academic work, *The Hope of the Great Community* (1916), was written at a time when the world appeared to be in great distress. The first World War was under way, the Lusitania had been sunk, and the international community was in disarray and upheaval. This book addressed the issues that had a profound effect on Royce at this time—the moral responsibilities and duties of the world community in relation to the events that were taking place.

Royce specifically discussed the concept of responsibility in relation to American politicians, the international community, and in his words, "the great community". The major underlying premise of this work deals with the notion that modern technology and science can usher in a new era of humanity that will overcome great tragedy and move us toward a humane world. His second main idea in here centered around the notion that the world would become an international community one day, and when this happened, both the international community and the individual nations would work together to preserve the ever-larger "great community".

The final academic publications of Royce's career were published posthumously. Of those publications, one set of articles is of particular interest to this research on Royce's contribution to symbolic interactionist thought. The articles are "Error and Truth," "Mind," "Monotheism," "Negation," and "Order." These five articles appeared in Hasting's *Encyclopaedia of Religion and Ethics* from 1912–1916. The article that most relevant to this research is "Mind" (1916).

In this article, Royce laid out his basic theory of the process of interpretation by summing up his ideas from previous publications. The beginning of "Mind," (1916) starts off with a history of the classical debate on whether all knowledge is perceptual (Henri Bergson) or conceptual (Plato). After having discussed the pitfalls of limiting cognitive knowledge to a situation of either/or, He decided that a synthesis of both types of knowledge was necessary, and addressed it in terms of a pragmatist view. Overall, Royce disagreed with the then-popular pragmatist synthesis of both perceptual and conceptual knowledge because it fell short of explaining interpretation. This lack for accountability of the interpretive process prompted him to formulate his own theory of perceptual and conceptual knowledge that not only permitted interpretation as a process but also emphasized its internal and external nature.

Concluding Thoughts

The ten major works and posthumously published articles discussed throughout this chapter represent the bulk of the academic writings of Royce. The point of systematically laying out his work goes back to two main goals of this study stated earlier: to establish the dates and times in which Royce produced academic works, and to place Royce's academic work within the larger context of the writings of James, Peirce, and Dewey and the socio-historical time period within which they all wrote and lived.

While the history of the writings of James, Dewey, and Peirce in the introduction was in no way exhaustive, the inclusion of their major books and articles in reference to when Royce produced his major academic works produced the following dualistic desired effect. First, in terms of time frame or historical reference, there appears to be little or no gap between the contributions of the four American pragmatists were publishing. Each individual person, whether it be James, Dewey, Peirce, or Royce, had his major academic breakthrough during the 1885–1890 time period. This fact reinforces the idea that Royce's writings did *not* predate or exist before the formative years of the other major American pragmatists.

Second, the complete survey of all of Royce's academic works in relation to the writings of the other pragmatists makes another point. Since Royce's later writings were published during the 1912–1916 timeframe, he did *not* exist outside of or postdate the other pragmatists. Because the overall point here is that, because Royce published his later works near the same time as the other pragmatists and died fairly close to both James and Peirce, his works do not postdate the later development of pragmatic thought.

These two points are significant to the research at hand because as Reynolds states, "if forced to single out the one philosophical school of thought that most influenced symbolic interactionism, one would be on safe ground in concluding that pragmatism provides its primary intellectual underpinnings" (1993, 13). In this sense, pragmatic thought was the lead instigator in the formation of early symbolic interactionism. Overall, this means that not only did Royce write, think, and publish as a pragmatist during the same time period as the other pragmatic giants of the early movement, but it also means that he would have developed ideas that can be found in both Mead's early and Blumer's later and more current symbolic interactionist thought.

In summary, by creating a survey of the academic work of Royce and overlaying it against the work of the other early American pragmatists, four definite statements can be made. First, the academic works of Royce did *not* predate the early formative years of the philosophy of pragmatism; second, Royce created and published academic works at the *same time* as the other early American pragmatists, meaning that he did *not* miss the crucial developmental years; third, considering the time in which Royce wrote and lived in comparison with James, Dewey, and Peirce, Royce did *not* postdate or exist after the later development of pragmatic thought; and fourth, the fact that Royce's academic works do not predate or postdate the height of the pragmatic movement suggests that by analyzing his philosophy and social theory, we can see if they contain substantive elements of early and later symbolic interactionist thought.

CHAPTER II

ROYCEAN IDEAS ON PERCEPTION, CONCEPTION, AND INTERPRETATION

The Problem of Christianity (1913) represents one of Royce's major academic works. Royce attempts "to show the need to understand religious beliefs in terms of a general theory of the nature of things and the types of beings there are" (Royce 1968, 2). Royce is able to accomplish this task by carefully examining Christian beliefs while placing them in a more modern context through the use of philosophical and scientific concepts. Within the theological, philosophical, and scientific concepts used in this book, there is the theme of how interpretation plays an integral role in humans' everyday lives. The theme of interpretation that Royce describes within the later chapters of this book provides a myriad of symbolic interactionist connections. That is the reason a summary of Chapters 11-14 is presented below.

  For Royce, the term "interpretation" is not solely important to philosophers and those in the academy. Instead, he views interpretation, or the process of interpretation, as being an everyday instance—a commonality of living life as a human. Royce gives an example of interpretation's utility when he states that "when a stranger in a foreign land desires the services of an interpreter, when a philologist offers his rendering of a text, when a judge construes a statute, some kind of interpretation is in question" (Royce 1968, 273). In addition to seeing interpretation as an everyday occurrence, Royce sees the "process of interpretation, as intending to meet human needs which are as well-known as they are vital; such needs determine, as we shall see, whatever is humane and articulate in the whole conduct and texture of our lives" (Royce 1968, 273). In this sense, interpretation is not only vital and necessary to our lives, but it also exists within our very fabric.

After having emphasized interpretation's overall importance in our lives, Royce goes on to posit the major question: "What is an interpretation?" (Royce 1968, 274). Royce here admits that "the process of interpretation takes us at once to the very heart of philosophy, throws a light both on the oldest and on the latest issues of metaphysical thought" (Royce 1968 274). For Royce, the key lies beneath centuries of classical philosophical thought. Royce then begins an overview of perceptual and conceptual knowledge and details its history within philosophy starting with Plato and ending with Kant.

In classical philosophy, there is a major debate over whether all cognitive knowledge is based upon conceptual or perceptual knowledge. Royce views this debate as being "the contrast between the cognitive processes called, respectively, perception and conception, as dominating a great part of the history of philosophy" (Royce 1968, 277). This dualistic debate on human cognition, according to Royce's outline, concerns three viewpoints: Plato's (conceptual), Bergson's (perceptual), and Kant's (synthesis).

Plato believed that all knowledge is conceptual or "knowledge of universals, of relations, or of other such 'abstract' objects" (Royce 2001, 57), which makes up all of our cognitive processes. The opposite viewpoint on this debate comes from French philosopher Bergson, who viewed human cognition as being solely based upon perception or immediate experience. While both philosophers make arguments for their side of the debate, Royce could not envision human cognition as being based upon an either/or situation.

This murky classical debate between Plato's conceptual world and Bergson's perceptual one becomes irrelevant to Royce, who informs us that, "despite this prevalence of the dual classification of our cognitive processes, most of us will readily acknowledge that, in our real life, we human beings are never possessed either of pure perception or of pure conception" (Royce 1968, 278). The importance of both perceptual and conceptual knowledge as a synthesis is emphasized when Royce says that, "Human knowledge is neither pure perception nor pure conception, but it always depends on the marriage of the two processes" (Royce 1968, 279).

Though Royce's investigation of perceptual and conceptual knowledge led him to believe in a dual-synthesized version of cognition, there is a piece of the proverbial puzzle that is missing. While "Many philosophers of otherwise widely different opinions recognize that conception and perception are, in life, cognitive processes brought into synthesis by some sort of activity, the activity of the mind whose cognitions are in question" (Royce 1968, 280) are that of interpretation or "knowledge of the third type". The point Royce is making in this quotation is the idea that, while perceptual and conceptual knowledge are synthesized, there must be a mental activity that brings this about. That activity is interpretation. Royce's explanation of a third cognitive process or "knowledge of the third type" begins with a discussion of Peirce's work in the area of interpretation. For Peirce, "Interpretation always involves a relation of three terms. In the technical phrase, interpretation *is* a triadic relation" (Royce 1968, 286). This statement is taken one step further when Peirce states that "You cannot express any complete process of interpreting by merely naming two terms, persons, or other objects, and by then telling what dyadic relation exists between one of these two and the other" (Royce 1968, 286).

An example of what Peirce and Royce are discussing is described in the example:

> Suppose that an Egyptologist translates an inscription. So far two beings are indeed in question: the translator and his text. But a genuine translation cannot be merely a translation in the abstract. There must be some language into which the inscription is translated. Let this translation be, in a given instance, an English translation. Then the translator interprets something: but he interprets it only to one who can read English (Royce 1968, 286).

For Peirce and Royce, if the person that requires the Egyptologist to translate the inscription to English does not understand the English language, there could not be an interpretation. This happens because, in the aforementioned situation, there would only be a dyad or two-way relationship—that of the Egyptian text and the Egyptologist who can translate. According to Peirce and Royce, there is a potential for interpretation to happen because interpretation consists of "a triad of beings—the Egyptian text, the Egyptologist who translates, and the possible English reader" (Royce 1968, 286). In this sense, interpretation is dependent upon the situation in which it occurs.

Regardless of the context or situation in which interpretation takes place, for Peirce and Royce, it will always consist of a threefold or triadic nature. This triadic formula involves "...the interpreter...the object-the person or the meaning or the text—which is interpreted; [and]...the person to whom the meaning is addressed" (Royce 1968, 287). An example of this triadic relation can be seen in the following example:

> You may observe that, when a man perceives a thing, the
> relation is dyadic. **A** perceives **B**. A pair of members is needed,
> and suffices, to make the relation possible. But when **A**
> interprets **B** to **C**, a triad of members (whereof, as in case or
> other relations, two or all three members may be wholly, or in
> part, identical) must exist in order to make the interpretation
> possible (Royce 1968, 287).

At first glance, this quotation may suggest that for something to be
interpreted, there must be three people; however, that is not the case. The
triadic model that Peirce and Royce discuss allows room for a conversation
of interpretations to exist because in many cases, we interpret the
meanings of our neighbors while sending out signs and symbols to be
interpreted ourselves.

Another reason that the triadic model of interpretation incorporates
alternative definitions of who an interpreter can be deals with the notion
that interpretation is both an external and internal process. Thus far, a
majority of the conversation has centered on interpretation as an external
process or a triadic model that focused on the world of interpretation that
happens only outside of the human mind. One major area that Royce and
Peirce pioneer in their theories of interpretation is the idea that
interpretation happens not only as an external process but also as an
internal process.

Royce gives an example of this internal process in the following passage:

> When a process of conscious reflection goes on, a man may be
> said to interpret himself. And, in general, in such a case, the
> man who is said to be reflecting remembers some former
> promise or resolve of his own, or perhaps reads an old letter
> that he once wrote, or an entry in a diary; he then, at some
> present time, interprets this expression of his past self (Royce
> 1968, 287).

Not only does a person reflect on his past, but for the person in this
example, he also "interprets past self to his future self. 'This,' he says, 'is
what I meant when I made that promise. 'This is what I wrote, recorded, or
promised. Therefore,' he continues, addressing his future self, 'I am now
committed to doing thus, planning thus' and so on" (Royce 1968, 287).

This example, though completely internal, still retains the triadic nature
of Peirce and Royce's idea because there is an interpreter, a meaning or
text, and someone to whom the meaning is addressed (in this case the
person who is having a conversation of ideas within his or her own mind).

For the person in this example, making promises based upon the past, present, and future definitely makes use of the triadic model. In Royce's example that "there are three men present in and taking part in the interior conversation: the man of the past whose promises, notes, records, or old letters, are interpreted; the present self who interprets them; and the future self to whom the interpretation is addressed" (Royce 1968, 287). The idea that interpretation is an internal process and external process is groundbreaking in that it creates a sound model by which to discuss and understand how interpretation works and functions in our daily lives.

Another perspective on the process of interpretation centers on the notion that interpretation is temporal (i.e., based upon past, present, and future experiences). For Royce, the process of interpretation is no different than that of a geologist studying a canyon in the desert. First, a geologist considers the canyon's age and its formation; essentially the canyon's past. Then, a geologist may look at its present condition to describe what has happened over a period of time. For example, the geologist may look for signs of physical and chemical weathering, current rock placement, rock formations, and water runoff. These factors would be considered the canyon's present. Finally, a geologist will consider all the factors looked at and determine what sort of measures need to be taken in the future to prevent further weathering, erosion, etc.; this is essentially the canyon's future. This same temporal process applies to humans and interpretation, "that is, we can define the present as, potentially, the interpretation of the past to the future" (Royce 1968, 289).

Toward the end of this chapter, Royce changed gears and switched his focus away from a philosophical explanation of interpretation toward an investigation of interpretation as a psychological process. For Peirce and Royce, interpretation and the triadic model represent more than "a mere logical formalism. Psychologically speaking, the mental process which thus involves three members differs from perception and conception in three respects" (Royce 1968, 289). The first point that Royce makes is that "interpretation is a conversation and not a lonely enterprise" (Royce 1968, 289). This point illustrates the idea that "there is someone in the realm of psychological happenings who addresses someone. The one who addresses interprets some object to the addressed" (Royce 1968, 289).

From this argument, Royce makes a second observation: "The interpreted object is itself something which has the nature of a mental expression. Peirce uses the term "sign" to name this mental object which is interpreted" (Royce 1968, 289). This led to Royce's final point. "Since interpretation is a mental act, and is an act which is expressed, the interpretation itself is, in its turn, a sign. This new sign calls for further interpretation, for the interpretation is addressed to somebody. And so, at the least in ideal, the social process involved is endless" (Royce 1968, 289). For Peirce and Royce, the three aspects of interpretation as a mental/psychological process allow a "formal character of a situation wherein any interpretation takes place" (Royce 1968, 290).

This mental/psychological explanation of interpretation and the interpretive process greatly differs from perception and conception as mental processes. On one hand, perception as a mental process "has its natural terminus in some object perceived; and therewith the process, as would seem, might end, where there is nothing else in the world to perceive" (Royce 1968, 290). On the other hand, conception "is contented, so to speak, with defining the universal type, or ideal form from which chances to become an object of somebody's thought. In order to define a new universal, one needs a new act of thought whose occurrence seems, in so far, an arbitrary additional cognitive function" (Royce 1968, 290).

In this sense, perception and conception are essential cognitive functions even though "both are, so to speak, self-limiting processes" (Royce 1968, 290). This is where interpretation distinguishes itself as being quite different from perception and conception; it is not a limited process.

Interpretation does not suffer from the limitations of perception and conception because it "requires as its basis the sign or mental expression which is to be interpreted, and calls for further interpretation of its own act, just because it addresses itself to some third being" (Royce 1968, 290). This ongoing process of interpretation "is not only an essentially social process, but also a process which, when once initiated, can be terminated only by an external and arbitrary interruption, such as death or social separation" (Royce 1968, 290). This vastly differs from perception and conception because both of those cognitive processes can stop, though often for only a limited time. While the process of interpretation, "calls, in ideal, for an infinite sequence of interpretations" (Royce 1968, 290). Thus, interpretation plays an integral part in human cognition as an infinite sequence of events.

In summary, Chapter 11 in *The Problem of Christianity* (1913) presented several new ideas on Royce's theory of the process of interpretation. Contained at the end of the chapter, Royce provides an overview of the eight main points of his lecture:

First, "In addition to the world of conception and to the world of perception, we have to take into account a *world of interpretation*" (Royce 1968, 291).

Second, "The features that distinguish one from one another of the three processes; perception, conception, and interpretation have to do with their logical and formal characteristics, with their psychological motives and accompaniments, and with the objects to which they are directed" (Royce 1968 291).

Third, "Logically and formally considered, interpretation differs from perception and from conception by the fact that it involves relations which are *essentially triadic*" (Royce 1968, 294).

Fourth, "Psychologically, interpretation differs from perception and conception by the fact that it is, in its intent, an essentially *social* process" (Royce 1968 294).

Fifth, "Both logically and psychologically, interpretation differs from perception and from conception in that each of these latter processes derives the wealth of its facts from a world which, at least in seeming, is *external to itself*" (Royce 1968, 294).

Sixth, "In this world of interpretation, of whose most general structure we have now obtained a glimpse, selves and communities may exist, past and future can be defined, and the realms of the spirit may find a place which neither barren conception nor the chaotic flow of interpenetrating perceptions could ever render significant" (Royce 1968, 294).

Seventh, "The interpretations of life which send us across the borders of both our conceptual and perceptual life, to lay up treasures in other words, to interpret the meaning of the processes of time, to read the meaning of art and of life" (Royce 1968, 295).

The eighth and final point is that interpretation "is the process which you engage whenever you take counsel with a friend, or look in the eyes of one beloved, or serve the cause of your life. This process (interpretation) is that which touches the heart of reality" (Royce 1968, 295).

CHAPTER III

ROYCEAN IDEAS ON THE
WILL TO INTERPRET

Chapter twelve in *The Problem of Christianity* (1913) begins with a discussion on the relative value of interpretation as a process. This discussion is a necessity, for as Royce said, "If I am right, and interpretation is indeed a fundamental cognitive process, we shall need still further to illustrate its nature and its principal forms" (Royce 1968, 297). In order for Royce to examine the nature and forms of the interpretative process, he splits his discussion into two main parts: "First, we shall study the elementary psychology of the process of interpretation…Secondly, we shall portray the ideal that guides a truth loving interpreter" (Royce 1968, 298). It is the first main part that will be the focus of this chapter.

Royce begins his discussion of interpretation by stating that "I have called interpretation an essentially social process; and such, in fact, it is. Man is an animal that interprets; and therefore, man lives in communities, and depends upon them for insight" (Royce 1968, 298). This being said, Royce decided that for his discussion on the topic of the elementary psychological forms of interpretation, he was going to look beyond whether interpretation is an individual or group process. Instead, his focus was on "the need to consider how an interpreter conducts his mental processes, even when he is taking no explicit account of other minds than his own" (Royce 1968, 298).

In looking for the mental processes of the interpreter, Royce went back to using the philosophical concepts and ideas of Peirce. One concept that Royce employs in his psychological discussion involves Peirce's "formal definition of the mental functions which are involved" (Royce 1968, 298) in interpretation as a process. For Peirce, "whenever an interpretation takes place, however little, it seems to be an explicit social undertaking, a triadic cognitive process can be observed" (Royce 1968, 298). Peirce takes this idea one step further by stating that "every instance of conscious and explicit comparison involves an elementary form of interpretation" and the same triadic model (Royce 1968, 298).

This observation by Peirce "enables us to study interpretation in some of its simplest shapes, relieved of the complications which our social efforts to communicate with other minds usually involve" (Royce 1968, 298). Royce used Peirce's concepts and ideas to allow "us to look, then, for elementary instances of such a triadic process"—the triadic process of mental comparison (Royce 1968, 298).

According to Royce, "most instances of the mental process known as comparison seem, at first sight, to consist of a consciousness of certain familiar dyadic relations, relations of similarity and difference" (Royce 1968, 299). For example, the color purple is offset by the color bright yellow, and "sound breaks in upon silence" (Royce 1968, 299). In this sense, "one sensory quality collides, as it were, with another and this shock difference awakens our attention" (Royce 1968, 299). However, "in other cases, an unexpected similarity of colors and tones attracts our interest or perhaps the odors of two flowers, or the flavors of two fruits, resemble one another" (Royce 1968, 299). The pairs of objects mentioned in each of these examples "are perceived objects, which in all these cases, fall into question" (Royce 1968, 299). We can express this problem of comparison philosophically by stating that "our observations in such judgments are: '**A** resembles **B**;' and '**D** is unlike **E**'" (Royce 1968, 299).

Royce takes Peirce's ideas on comparison one step further by creating his own definition: "Comparison, in the fuller sense of the word, takes place when one asks or answers the questions: *What* constitutes the difference between **A** and **B**? *Wherein* does **A** resemble **B**? *Wherein* consists their distinction?" (Royce 1968, 299). Royce illustrates this definition by using an example:

> If you write a word with your own hand, and hold it up before a mirror, your own handwriting becomes more or less unintelligible to you, unless you are already accustomed to read or to write mirror-script. Suppose, however, that instead of writing words yourself, you let someone else show you words already written. And suppose, further, that two words have been written side by side on the same sheet of paper, neither of them by your own hand. Suppose one of them to have been written upright, while the other is the counter part of the first, except that it is the first turned upside down, or else is the first in mirror-script (Royce 1968, 299).

In this example, the person who is looking at the words produced should be able to distinguish that the words are seemingly different. Yet they also have a close resemblance to one another. However, "unless you were already familiar with the results of inverting a handwriting or of observing it in a mirror, you could not thus directly observe wherein consist the similarities and the differences of the two words which lie before you on the paper" (Royce 1968, 299). Since we are knowledgeable of how mirror-script works in conjunction with the end result of turning paper upside down, there should be no problem in identifying the difference of the two words.

Yet as Royce argues "in order to compare the two words thus presented side by side on the same sheet of paper, and to tell wherein they are similar and wherein they differ, you need what Peirce calls a 'mediating idea,' or what he calls 'a third,' which, as he phrases the matter, shall 'represent' or 'interpret' one of the two written words to, or in terms, of, the other" (Royce 1968, 300). According to Royce, people use Peirce's concept of "a third" when they make statements like "This word is the mirror-script representative of that word" (1968, 300). Phrases and comments such as these made about the word written in the mirror-script and the differences between the two words as written illustrate that "the actual differences between the words are interpreted" (Royce 1968, 300).

An alternative explanation about comparison is that "a complete act of comparison involves a 'third,' a 'mediating' image or idea, and an 'interpreter.' By means of this 'third,' you so compare a 'first' object with a 'second' as to make clear to yourself wherein consists the similarity and the difference between the second and the first" (Royce 1968, 300). In this sense, "comparison must be triadic in order to be both explicit and complete" (Royce 1968, 300). This applies to the example of the mirror-script because Royce states that "likenesses and differences are the signs that a comparison is needed" (Royce 1968, 300). Though this may be true, that likenesses and differences can be signs, Royce reminds us that "these signs are not their own interpretation" (1968, 300).

Another type of comparison that Royce discussed deals with the issue of comparing "how" two things are alike or different. More specifically, Royce investigated the question "How does **A** differ from **C**? If you can reply to this question by saying that, by means of **B**, **A** can be altogether transformed into **C**, or can, at least, be brought into a close resemblance to **C**, then the comparison of **A** to **C** is made definite" (Royce 1968, 302). Royce presented an example of this:

If you cut a strip of paper, -perhaps an inch wide and ten inches long, you can bring the two ends together and fasten them with glue. The result will be a ring-strip of paper, whose form is of a type very familiar in case of belts, finger-rings, and countless other objects. Before bringing the ends of the strip together, let one end of the paper be turned 180 degrees. Holding the twisted end of the strip fast, glue it to the other" (1968, 302).

You should now hold in your hand "an endless strip of paper having in it a single twist (Royce 1968, 302). Now lay the single twisted strip of paper next to a strip of untwisted paper. Next, "ask a person who has not seen you make the two ring-strips, to compare them, and to tell you wherein they agree and wherein they differ" (Royce 1968, 302). If you asked this question to an ordinary passerby who is not familiar with why you cut the ring-strips, that person will answer the question by saying that "they obviously differ because one of them has no twist in it, while the other certainly has some kind of twist belonging to its structure". The person making this comparison of the ring-strips uses Peirce's idea of a "third" idea; however, it will take the person making this comparison some time to "make his comparison at all complete and explicit" (Royce 1968, 302).

To make his comparison explicit, the ring-strip observer may need to have his or her attention called to "the fact that the ring-strip which contains the single twist has two extraordinary properties: It has, namely, but one side; and it also has but one edge" (Royce 1968, 302). At first, your observer will be astounded at this fact because he or she has not considered the ring-strip in such great detail. When the observer considers the ring-strip situation more closely, he or she "will find that the idea of a 'one-sided strip of paper' enables him or her to compare the new and the old forms, and to interpret his idea of the new ring form to his old idea of an ordinary ring which has no twist, and possesses two sides" (Royce 1968, 302).

Thus far "in all the cases of explicit comparison which we have just considered, what takes place has, despite the endless varieties of circumstance, a uniform character" (Royce 1968, 303). For Royce, this uniform character is the underlying principle that "whoever compares has before him what we have called two distinct ideas; either his ideas of the two printed or written words, or again, his ideas of the two ring-strips of paper" (Royce 1968, 303). Regardless of the example, the process of comparison requires two distinct ideas.

Peirce views the process of comparison in a similar manner. For him, the process of comparison requires us to make "an explicit comparison, which provides us with two distinct and contrasting ideas. It is their distinctiveness, and it is their contrast, which determines our task" (Royce 1968, 303). The ideas contained within a comparison not only have both perceptual and conceptual aspects, but they also have "different and sometimes conflicting 'leadings,' different and sometimes mutually estranged motives, activities, or constructions" (Royce 1968, 303). These two different sets of ideas have a contrast between them such as with pieces of artwork, or there may be one comparison that might stand out amongst the other as in the case of a rectangle in comparison with a triangle.

Though Royce and Peirce share in their overall views about the "process of comparison" and the notion of "a third," there is a bone of contention between the two philosophers. For Royce, "the essential fact for our present study is that, in the case of the comparisons which Peirce discusses, the problem, whether you call it a theoretical or practical problem, is not that of linking percepts to their fitting concepts, nor that of paying the bank bills of conception in the gold of the corresponding perceptions" (Royce 1968, 304). The real problem, according to Royce, "is the problem either of arbitrating the conflicts or of bringing to mutual understanding the estrangements; or of uniting in some community the separated lives of these two distinct ideas, ideas which, when left to themselves, decline to coalesce or to cooperate, or to enter into one life" (1968, 304).

This problem for Peirce can be solved simply by having a person participate in a new act. For Peirce, "this new act consists in the invention or discovery of some third idea, distinct from both the ideas which are to be compared. This third idea, when once found interprets one of the ideas which are the objects of the comparison and interprets it to the other or in the light to the other" (Royce 1968, 304). The version of the process of comparison that Peirce describes because of its "complexity and the significance of the processes involved require further study" (Royce 1968, 304). For Royce to further investigate Peirce's ideas on the process of comparison, he asks the question "What is to be gained by the sort of comparison which Peirce characterizes" (Royce 1968, 304)?

Royce answers this question by first examining the heart of Peirce's concepts and ideas involving the process of comparison. According to Royce, Peirce's version of the interpretive process or his "concept of interpretation, in general, defines an extremely general process" (Royce 1968, 305). Peirce's process of comparison is considered general by Royce because "Peirce's theory of comparison is quite as well illustrated by purely mathematical as by explicitly social instances" (Royce 1968, 305). In addition, Peirce shows "no essential inconsistency between the logical and psychological motives which lie at the basis of his theory of the triad of interpretation" (Royce 1968, 305).

This is not to say that Royce believes Peirce's work holds little relevance on the topic of comparison. In fact, it's quite the opposite; however, for Royce, we must move beyond Peirce's simplistic model of comparison and interpretation. To accomplish this, Royce asks a new question: "But a comparison of ideas that, too, is no doubt an active process. To what does it lead? It leads, as we have seen, to a new, to a third, to an interpreting idea. And what is this new idea? What does it present to our view" (Royce 1968, 305)?

According to Royce, "one must first answer this question in a very old-fashioned way" (Royce 1968, 305). The examples of comparison discussed earlier (mirror-script and paper strips) were not only investigations into interpretation but also Peirce's concept of "a third." These examples, though found in everyday life, also "show us, ourselves, and also create a new grade of clearness regarding what we are and what we mean" (Royce 1968, 305). This happens, according to Royce, because "the new or third idea shows us ourselves, as we are. Next, it also enriches our world of self-consciousness. It at once broadens our outlook and gives our mental realm definiteness and self-control. It teaches one of our ideas what another of our ideas means" (Royce 1968, 305). In sum, comparison allows humans to "know our right hand from our left hand; how to connect what comes to us in fragments; how to live as if life has some coherent aim" (Royce 1968, 305).

Royce takes his ideas on comparison one step further when he looks at perception and conception in relation to the comparative process. Many of the philosophers of Royce's time taught comparative knowledge and "self-knowledge as being either intuitive or perceptual (merely fluent or transient) or conceptual (abstract and sterile)" (Royce 1968, 306). Royce challenged this dualistic view because "a dual antithesis between perceptual and conceptual knowledge is once and for all inadequate to explain the wealth of the facts of life" (Royce 1968, 306). For Royce, "When you accomplish an act of comparison, the knowledge which you attain is neither merely conceptual, nor perceptual, nor yet merely a practical active synthesis of perception and conception" (1968, 306). Instead, comparison involves "a third type of knowledge" (Royce 1968, 306); it involves interpretation.

From this point on, Royce changes and moves toward investigating interpretation and comparison as part of a more social process. This movement toward the social process is indicated when Royce states that "one who compares a pair of his own ideas may attain, if he is successful, that vision of unity, that grade of self-possession, which we have now illustrated. But one who undertakes to interpret his neighbor's ideas is in a different position" (1968, 312).

Interpreting your neighbor's ideas differs from Royce's earlier example of comparison because "an interpreter, in his social relations with other men, deals with two different minds, neither of which he identifies with as his own. His interpretation is a 'third' or mediating idea. This concept/idea of a 'third' is aroused in the interpreter's mind through signs which come to him from the mind that he interprets" (Royce 1968, 312). Humans address this concept of a third "to the mind to which interprets the first" (Royce 1968, 312). The distinctions made on the process of interpretation and comparison made in this chapter are important to Royce because "the psychology of the process of social interpretation, so far as that process goes on in the interpreter's individual mind, is identical with the psychology of comparison which we have now outlined" (Royce 1968, 312-313).

The reason that the "process of interpretation" and the "process of comparison" outlined in this chapter share numerous commonalities centers on Royce's formulated idea that "Nobody can interpret, unless the idea which he interprets has become more or less clearly and explicitly one of his own ideas, and unless he compares it with another idea which is, in some sense, his own" (Royce 1968, 313). However, "from the point of view of the interpreter, the essential difference between the case where he is interpreting the mind of one of his neighbors to the mind of another neighbor, and the case wherein he is comparing two ideas of his own, is a difference in the clearness of vision which is, under human conditions, attainable" (Royce 1968, 313).

When someone takes two ideas that are internally his or hers and decides to compare them, that individual is participating in the successful completion of the interpretive process. This internal process, though only lasting temporarily, creates a model by which to make further interpretations; however, this changes "when we endeavor to interpret your neighbor's mind, because your interpretation has to remain remote from its goal" (Royce 1968, 313).

Meaning that "my neighbor's ideas I indeed in a measure grasp, and compare with other ideas, and interpret; but, as I do this, I see through a glass darkly. Only those ideas whose comparisons with other ideas, and whose resulting triadic interpretations I can view face-to-face, can appear to me to have become in a more intimate and complete sense of my own individual ideas" (Royce 1968, 313).

Another way in which to consider this would be: "Under ordinary social conditions this other mind is viewed as the mind of my neighbor. Neither my neighbor nor myself have any direct intuition. But of my own ideas I can hope to win the knowledge which the most successful comparisons exemplify" (Royce 1968, 313). Royce provides an example of this situation:

> I, the interpreter, regard you, my neighbor, as a realm of ideas, of 'leadings,' of meanings, of pursuits, of purposes. This realm is not wholly strange and incomprehensible to me. For at any moment, in my life as an interpreter, I am dependent upon the results of countless previous efforts to interpret. The whole past history of civilization has resulted in that form and degree of interpretation of you and of other fellow men which I already possess, at any instant when I begin afresh the task of interpreting your life or your ideas. You are to me, then, a realm of ideas which lie outside of the centre which my will to interpret can momentarily illumine with the clearest grade of vision (1968, 314).

This example of comparing and interpreting the ideas of your neighbor is not the end of Royce's ideas on the subject. In fact, he takes the process of interpretation and the process of comparison one step further. For him, interpretation and comparison on a larger level reflects a need for a community of interpretation/comparison. Since humans are constantly engaged in the process of interpreting and comparing one another, Royce creates the idea of a community of interpretation. The community of interpretation is defined thusly:

> Since the same will to interpret you is also expressive of my analogous interests in all my other neighbors, what I here and now specifically aim to do is this: I mean to interpret you to somebody else, to some other neighbor, who is neither yourself nor myself. Three of us, then, I seek to bring into the desired unity of interpretation (1968, 314).

This community of interpretation is triadic according to Royce: "If, then, I am worthy to be an interpreter at all, we three, you, my neighbor, whose mind I would fain interpret, you, my kindly listener, to whom I am to address my interpretation, we three constitute a Community. Let us give this community a technical name, let us call it a *Community of Interpretation*" (1968, 315).

CHAPTER IV

THE ROYCEAN CONCEPT
OF THE "DOCTRINE OF SIGNS"

Chapter fourteen of *The Problem of Christianity*, (1913) titled "Doctrine of Signs," concluded Royce's major discussion on the concept of interpretation and the triadic model. In this chapter, Royce changed his focus from interpretation to Peirce's theory of signs. Peirce's theory of signs plays a significant part in Royce's final conclusions about interpretation, society, and the universe in general.

The chapter begins with an overview of Peirce's theory of signs. For Peirce, the actual term "sign" is defined as "the name for an object to which somebody gives or should give an interpretation" (Royce 1968, 344). This definition, though direct in its meaning, does not cover all the bases in terms of what "signs" can represent. For example, "a sign can be something that determines an interpretation" (Royce 1968, 345), yet it can "also be called an expression of a mind; and, in our social intercourse, it actually is such an expression" (Royce 1968, 345). In addition, "one might say that a sign is, in its essence, either a mind or a quasi-mind—an object that fulfills the function of a mind" (Royce 1968, 345).

These different manifestations of the meaning and representation of the term "sign" serve a purpose. The concept "sign" needs to be applicable in everyday situations; "thus, a word, a clock-face, a weather-vane, or a gesture is a sign" (Royce 1968, 345). Besides being applicable to everyday life, a "sign" also "expresses a mind, and it calls for an interpretation through some other mind, which shall act as mediator between the sign, or between the maker of the sign, and someone to whom the sign is to be read" (Royce 1968, 345). In addition, according to Royce, interpreting a "sign" "is, in its turn, the expression of the interpreter's mind, it constitutes a new sign, which again calls for interpretation; and so on without end; unless the process is arbitrarily interrupted" (1968, 345).

From these meanings and representations of the concept "sign," Royce creates his own definition for the concept. "A sign, then, is an object whose being consists in the fact that the sign calls for an interpretation" (Royce 1968, 345). The difference between Peirce's conception of "sign" and Royce's understanding of the concept is based on a disagreement of usage. For Peirce, "sign" is part of a logical formalism because his use of the concept was designed for logic, while Royce's definition of "sign" is based closely upon the study of metaphysics or his metaphysical thesis that "the universe consists of real signs and of their interpretation" (Royce 1968, 345); a thesis that Royce investigated more closely.

For Royce, "in the order of real time the events of the world are signs. They are followed by interpreters, or by acts of interpretation which our own experience constantly exemplifies. For we live, as selves, by interpreting the events and the meaning of our experience. History consists of such interpretations" (Royce 1968, 345). Each one of these acts requires an interpretation, which "in turn, is expressed, in the order of time, by new signs. The sequence of these signs and interpretations constitutes the history of the universe" (Royce 1968, 346).

Royce reiterates this point by stating that "whatever our experiences exemplify, our metaphysical doctrine of signs generalizes to the world at large" (Royce 1968, 346). We must keep in mind that the point Royce makes is not by any means brand new, and he gives proper credit to Bergson for originating the notion that "the world of any present moment of time is a summary of the results of all past experiences" (Royce 1968, 346). While Royce is not the originator of the past-to-present thesis, he does create a new conceptualization on this earlier idea. He is able to do this "since any idea, and especially any antithesis or contrast of ideas, is, according to our metaphysical thesis, a sign, which in the world finds its real interpretation, our metaphysical theory maybe called a 'doctrine of signs'" (Royce 1968, 346).

In summary, the "doctrine of signs," according to Royce, is "the very being of the universe and it consists of a process whereby the world is interpreted—not indeed in its wholeness, at any one moment of time, but in and through an infinite series of acts of interpretation" (Royce 1968, 346). The infinite series Royce described makes up both the temporal order (past, present, and future) and all of its intricacies and complexities.

In addition, "the temporal order is an order of purposes and of deeds, simply because it is the essence of every rational deed to be an effort to interpret a past life to a future life; while every act of interpretation aims to introduce unity into life, by mediating between mutually contrasting or estranged ideas, minds and purposes" (Royce 1968, 346). In essence, our world, the temporal world, "in its wholeness, constitutes in itself an infinitely complex sign" (Royce 1968, 346). This complex sign that Royce discusses "as a whole, is interpreted to an experience which itself includes a synoptic survey of the whole of time" (Royce 1968, 346).

At first glance, Royce's "doctrine of signs" seems very philosophical and bound to metaphysics alone; however, that is not the case. A practical illustration of Royce's "doctrine of signs" can be seen in the following illustration. "When you observe, at a crossing of roads, a sign-post, you will never discover what the real sign-post is, either by continuing to perceive it, or by merely conceiving its structure or its relations to any perceived objects, or to any merely abstract laws in heaven or in earth" (Royce 1968, 346). In addition, you cannot "learn what the sign-post is by any process of watching in the course of your individual experience the 'workings' of any ideas that it suggests to you as this individual man" (Royce 1968, 347). The only way in which you can understand the sign-post is "if you learn to read it" (Royce 1968, 347). Not only must you learn to read, but you must also consider that the "very being of a sign-post consists in its nature as a guide, needing interpretation, and pointing the way" (Royce 1968, 347).

The signpost that Royce describes is easily recognizable as "real" (or real as based upon our perceptions); however, still needs to be interpreted. This process of interpretation, as Royce has illustrated in previous chapters, is triadic in nature, hence the interpretation of the signpost is no different. The signpost in this illustration is "constituted of at least three distinct minds" (Royce 1968, 347): first, there is "the mind whose intention to point out the way is expressed in the construction of the sign-post" (Royce 1968, 347); second, "there is the mind to which the sign-post actually points out the way," however, the sign's meaning is not made clear to this mind unless he or she knows how to read (Royce 1968, 347); third, "there must be a third mind which interprets the sign-post to the inquiring wayfarer (traveler). The wayfarer (traveler), if he knows how to read, may be his own interpreter" (Royce 1968, 347).

Royce takes his example of the signpost in relation to the "doctrine of signs" one step further when he considers the "three distinct mental functions" or "three minds" involved in interpreting the signpost. First, there's the "the function of the mind whose purpose the sign expresses" (Royce 1968, 347). Second, "there is the mind which is guided by the interpretation of the sign" (Royce 1968, 347). And lastly, there "is the function of the interpreter to whom the reading of the sign is due" (Royce 1968, 347).

The illustration of the signpost and the complex process of interpreting the meaning of the sign holds within it a larger commentary on life; it represents an illustration of Royce's "doctrine of signs." For Royce, "our experience, as it comes to us, is a realm of signs. That is, the facts of experience resemble signposts. You can never exhaustively find out what they are by resorting either to perception or to conception" (Royce 1968, 347).

This statement holds true for Royce, because "no working, of any single idea can show what a real fact of experience is. For a fact of experience, as you actually view that fact, is first an event belonging to an order of time— an event preceded by an infinite series of facts whose meaning it summarizes, and leading to an infinite series of coming events, into whose meaning it is yet to enter" (Royce 1968, 347).

Royce takes this notion of "a fact of experience" one step further, claiming that "the past and future of our real experiences are objects neither of pure perception nor of pure conception. Nor can you, at any present moment, verify any present idea of yours about any past event. Nor can you define past and future in terms of the present workings of any ideas" (Royce 1968, 348). The reason we cannot understand our ideas in terms of the current temporal world is because "past time and future time are known solely through interpretations. Past time we regard as real, because we view our memories as signs, which need and possess their interpretations" (Royce 1968, 348). This also means the following:

> Our expectations are interpreted to our future selves by our present deeds and therefore we regard our experiences as signs of the future. Therefore, to a being who merely perceived or conceived, or who lived wholly in the present workings of his ideas, past time and future time would be as meaningless as the sign-post would be to the wayfarer (traveler) who could not read, and who found nobody to interpret to him its meaning (Royce 1968, 348).

This statement brings Royce's theory of the "doctrine of signs" full circle, for his doctrine "extends to all reality the presuppositions which we use in all our dealings with past and future time" (Royce 1968, 348). In addition, Royce's "doctrine of signs" views "our memories as signs of the past and our expectations as signs of the future" (Royce 1968, 348).

To summarize this "doctrine of signs," Royce makes the following statement:

Our metaphysical thesis generalizes the rules which constantly guide our daily interpretations of life. All contrasts of ideas, all varieties of experience, all the problems which finite experience possesses, are signs. The real world contains (so our thesis asserts) the interpreter of these signs, and the very being of the world consists in the truth of the interpretation which, in the whole realm of experience, these signs obtain (Royce 1968, 348).

In Chapter Fourteen, Royce also began a discussion on "knowledge about the self" and its important relation to the "doctrine of signs" and interpretation. According to Royce, "the most important part of my knowledge about myself is based upon knowledge that I have derived from the community (society) to which I belong. In particular, my knowledge about the socially expressive moments of my own organism is largely derived from what I learn through the testimony of my fellow men" (Royce 1968, 358). An illustration is then provided. "For instance, the appearance of my fellow's countenance is to me a sign of his mind. And signs of this type stand in the front rank of those facts of perception upon which my customary interpretation of his mind depends whenever he and I are in each other's presence" (Royce 1968, 358).

Royce further explained this point by stating that "as a fact, I know very little about my own facial expressions, except what I learn, if indeed I learn at all, through accepting as true certain reports of my neighbors regarding these facial expressions" (Royce 1968, 359). Of course, a person can look at their own face in the mirror and indirectly perceive their facial expressions; however, this yields no knowledge about "what my own changes of facial expression are" (Royce 1968, 359). Since people cannot rely on the facial expressions observed in the mirror, they have to interpret the signs of others. According to Royce, we have "spent years of our lives interpreting the signs which we have read as we looked at the countenances of other men" (1968, 359).

Though this example seems basic, it is "typical for the way in which we interpret the usual signs of one's mind which our neighbor gives to us" (Royce 1968, 359). This is in large part true because, as Royce says, "I never normally view my own organism in a perspective which is closely analogous to the perspective in which I constantly perceive the body and the movements of my fellow man" (Royce 1968, 359). Overall, since we cannot know ourselves through our own interpretations alone, "our most important knowledge about our own expressive movements comes to us at second hand. We learn how our own movements appear through the report of others" (Royce 1968, 359). Thus, the way we view our expressive moments and representations of ourselves, such as facial expressions, is predicated upon not just our own perspective but the perspectives of others.

Royce poses one last question: "Why do I postulate others' minds?" (Royce 1968, 360). He partially answers by stating, "I postulate your mind first, because, when you address me, by word or gesture, you arouse in me ideas which, by virtue of their contrast with my ideas, and by virtue of their own novelty and their unexpectedness, I know to be not any ideas of my own" (Royce 1968, 360). According to Royce, when someone's mind is approached by ideas that are not their own, "you first try, however you can, to interpret those ideas which are not yours" (Royce 1968, 360). This mental "process of interpretation" that all humans are constantly involved in starts when "new ideas...words and deeds...are suggested to me that actually require an interpretation" (Royce 1968, 360).

These new ideas, as they are incoming to the mind, require "an interpreter" and "an interpretation" (Royce 1968, 360). The interpreter of the incoming ideas serves the function of "mediating between the new ideas which your deeds have suggested to me, and the trains of ideas which I already call my own" (Royce 1968, 360). After having mediated between both sets of ideas, the interpreter:

> Would compare all these ideas, and would both observe and express wherein lay their contrast and its meaning...Now such an interpreter, mediating between two contrasting ideas or sets of ideas, and making clear their contrasts, their meaning, and their mutual relations, would be, by hypothesis, a *mind* (Royce 1968, 360).

For Royce, the creation of a mind through an internal mental process of interpretation gives a response to the original question of postulating one's mind. "The reason, then, for postulating your mind is that the ideas which your words and movements have aroused within me are not my own ideas, and cannot be interpreted in terms of my own ideas while I actually hold, as the fundamental hypothesis of my social consciousness, that all contrasts of ideas have a real interpretation and are interpreted" (Royce 1968, 361). The sheer magnitude of the importance of interpretation in its relation to the formation of an interpreting mind and the doctrine of signs is so great it leads Royce to make the claim that "if there is no interpreter, there is no interpretation. And, if there is no interpretation, there is no world whatsoever" (1968, 362).

CHAPTER V

ROYCE'S THEORY

OF THE HUMAN MIND

The article, "Mind," written in 1916, was published toward the very end of Royce's academic career. This appeared in James Hastings's *Encyclopedia of Religion and Ethics* (1917). This article outlines Royce's later ideas on problems in epistemology and reflects many of his ideas that link him to symbolic interactionism. This chapter summarizes the ideas and themes of this article.

"Mind" begins with a brief discussion of "perceptual and conceptual knowledge as a fundamental cognitive process" (Royce 2001, 56). For Royce, the definitions of perceptual and conceptual knowledge are derived from two thinkers: James and Peirce. James uses the term "knowledge of acquaintance" to refer to perception, and it basically means one's ability to perceive through the senses. For example, "in the simplest possible case one who listens to music has 'knowledge of acquaintance' in the music; the musician who listens in the light of his professional knowledge has not only 'knowledge of acquaintance', but also 'knowledge about'; he recognizes what changes of key take place and what rules of harmony are illustrated" (Royce 2001, 57). This notion of "knowledge about" refers to James's idea of conceptual knowledge or knowledge based on abstract concepts that require development.

Though similar in definitions, Peirce conceptualized perceptual and conceptual knowledge in a different manner. For Peirce, "the name 'perception' is used in psychology with special reference to the perceptions of the various senses" (Royce 2001, 56–57). While Royce's notion of conceptual knowledge is defined as "knowledge of universals, of relations, or of other such abstract objects" (Royce 2001, 57). Though more simplistic in his conceptualizations, both ideas provide us with a clear sense of what Royce meant by the terms perceptual and conceptual knowledge.

Having established what is meant by perceptual and conceptual knowledge, Royce finds the dualistic classification of knowledge troubling, especially in the area of science. He states that "while the distinction between perceptual and conceptual knowledge is of great importance in determining the distinction between the deductive and the inductive methods in the sciences, the classification of these two modes of cognition does not suffice to determine what constitutes the difference between inductive and deductive science" (Royce 2001, 58).

For instance, in deductive (conceptual) science, abstract concepts and ideas are applied to the scientific method to show validity. From the scientific method, models, maps, and diagrams illustrating the ideas can be designed. The same idea is true of research done in mathematics using the same deductive (conceptual) model. With this in mind, Royce states that "our knowledge concerning numbers, the operations of a mathematical science and similar cases form exceptionally good instances of what characterizes conceptual knowledge in its exact and developed form" (Royce 2001, 58). In essence, deductive science represents James's "knowledge about."

"In the inductive use of scientific methods, we find a more complicated union of the perceptual and conceptual types of knowledge" (Royce 2001, 58), according to Royce. Inductive science requires a synthesis of both types of knowledge, because the researcher is investigating abstract principles while also applying conceptual knowledge to the perceptual world. For instance, Newton's law of gravity started out as merely a hypothesis: an abstract idea, a piece of conceptual knowledge; however, "when the hypothesis is tested by comparing the predictions based upon it with experience, the test involves appealing to perceptual knowledge" (Royce 2001, 58), or "knowledge of acquaintance" at some point. This happened to Newton when he was hit on the head by an apple; the conceptual basis for gravity became fused with Newton's perceptual experience.

This difference between deductive and inductive science and its synthesis forces Royce to seriously question "this dual classification of the fundamental processes of cognition" (Royce 2001, 58). Hence, Royce asks two major questions concerning the two types of cognitive knowledge: What is "the relative value of these two cognitive processes" and what is "the degree to which, in our actual cognitive processes, or in ideal cognitive processes the two can ever be separated" (Royce 2001, 59)?

To answer the first question, Royce investigated the classical philosophical debate between Plato's world of pure conceptual knowledge and Bergson's idea of pure perceptual knowledge. On one hand, Plato argued that "conceptual knowledge gives truth; perceptual knowledge gives illusion or appearance" (Royce 2001, 59). On the other hand, Bergson "declared that, if we had unlimited perceptual knowledge, *i.e.*, 'knowledge of acquaintance' whose limits and imperfections we had no occasion to feel, because it had no limits and no imperfections, then conceptions could have no possible interest for us as cognitive beings" (Royce 2001, 59). While both philosophers make valid arguments for their respective positions, neither admitted that a synthesis of ideas was possible. This classical problem within epistemology concerned both the pragmatists and the idealists of the early nineteenth century, especially Royce.

The idea of humanity's cognitive processes being viewed philosophically as a mere problem of either/or that could be solved by taking the side of one extreme idea over another seemed to Royce and other philosophers as outdated. This point is made clear when Royce wrote "Of course all the philosophers admit that, in practice, our knowledge makes use of, and from moment to moment consists in, a union which involves both conceptual and perceptual processes" (Royce 2001, 59). In making this statement, Royce answers both of his earlier proposed questions: What is the relative value of these two cognitive processes? The answer is that conceptual and perceptual knowledge both have value. What is the degree to which the two can be separated? There is no either/or situation, because both perceptual and conceptual knowledge have uses within our everyday life.

It is from this reference point within epistemology (synthesized cognition) that Royce creates his initial arguments on the existence of "knowledge of the third type" or a "third cognition." The "third cognition" can be viewed simply as "interpretation through the comparison of ideas as a third fundamental cognitive process" (Royce 2001, 60). An alternate way of thinking about "third cognition" would be that the human mind makes use of perceptual and conceptual knowledge along with interpretation. For Royce, this process of interpretation happens:

> When a man understands a spoken or written word or sentence, what he perceives is some sign, or expression of an idea or meaning, which in general belongs to the mind of some fellow man. When this sign or expression is understood by the one who hears or who reads, what is made present to the consciousness of the reader or hearer may be any combination of perceptual or conceptual knowledge that chances to be in question...However, my 'grasping of his idea', consists neither in the percept of the sign nor in the concept of its object which the

sign arouses, but in my interpretation of the sign as an
indication of an idea which is distinct from any idea of mine
(Royce 2001, 60).

The process of interpretation that Royce described in this quotation
makes use of both perceptual and conceptual knowledge along with the
interpretation of signs and symbols. Royce's version of the "knowledge of
the third type" creates a triadic view of human cognition that functions
upon the interplay of perceptual, conceptual, and interpretive knowledge.
This conceptualization is in stark contrast to the stale and outdated
arguments of Plato and Bergson in which human cognitive functioning
was reduced to one view or the other. In addition to separating himself
from the classical philosophers, Royce was able to circumvent the
problem of an either/or situation because interpretative knowledge is not
designed to be merely another type of cognition—an add-on. Royce sees
"interpretation as a third type of knowledge which is closely interwoven
with perceptual and conceptual knowledge" (Royce 2001, 61).

Another major area in which Royce's triadic view of cognition differs
from previous philosophers and epistemologists centers on his
admittance that interpretive knowledge is socially based. Royce expresses
this view when he states that "interpretation is the knowledge of the
meaning of a sign. Such a knowledge is not a mere apprehension, nor yet a
conceptual process; it is the essential social process whereby the knower
at once distinguishes himself, with his own meanings, ideas, and
expressions, from some other self, and at the same time knows that these
selves have their contrasted meanings, while one of them at the moment
is expressing its meaning to the other" (Royce 2001, 63).

In this sense, cognitive knowledge and its interplay of perceptual,
conceptual, and interpretive knowledge is not merely based upon a single
person's individual thoughts or individual interpretations, a sort of
exclusively internal process. Instead, Royce challenges the traditional view
of cognitive processes only occurring as part of an internal individual
process and presents his triadic model of cognition as both an internal
and external—an ongoing process. The overall point Royce makes is that
an individual does not merely reflect and interpret his or her own signs,
symbols, meanings, or selves; rather, people are constantly engaged in
reflecting and interpreting their own world (internal) along with the rest of
society's members (external). The reason this occurs is because human
beings are constantly interacting with other members of their community
(society).

In addition to Royce's triadic model being both an internal and external ongoing process, he also suggests that participation within this process represents a simultaneous action. When Royce discusses how someone "with his own meanings, ideas, and expressions, from some other self, and at the same time [one] knows that these selves have their contrasted meanings, while one of them at the moment is expressing its meaning to the other" (Royce 2001, 63), there is no downtime or lag between the processes going on between both individuals. This type of simultaneity expressed in Royce's process of interpretation mimics the notion of a "razor's edge present" for two reasons: Both people involved in the interpretive process are creating and interpreting/understanding the meaning of signs and symbols, and as soon as something is interpreted for meaning or understanding, it is part of the past. Once an interpretation of ideas, signs, and symbols becomes part of the past, it must be reflected upon because people are constantly involved in the perceptual, conceptual, and interpretative process amongst one another.

Royce takes his cognitive triadic model one step further by asserting "that every interpretation has three aspects" (Royce 2001, 63). He believes that "when an interpretation takes place, there is an act B wherein a mental process A is interpreted, read, or rendered to a third mind" (Royce 2001, 64). An example of this situation can be found in something as simple as a high five. Suppose two children win a sack race at a local summer festival. In their excitement over their victory, one child high-fives the other child for a race well-run. In Royce's model, child #1 giving a high five would be an act (B); then child #2, because of the high five, would undergo a mental process (A) in which that child would assess what the high five meant. Once this process is completed, child #2 would then, in response, use interpretation to define the situation and potentially repeat this process by giving child #1 a high five.

The triadic nature of interpretation that Royce described was purposely made to be simplistic, because interpretation is seen (by Royce) as being ever-present and ongoing. He made this point when he stated that "every explicit process involving self-consciousness, involving a definite sequence of plans of action, and dealing with long stretches of time, has this threefold character" (Royce 2001, 64). Royce's simplification of the cognitive process of interpretation allows philosophers and symbolic interactionists to see that interpretation is continuous. Royce's triadic model of interpretation retains its ability to be both an internal and external process, just as an interpretation can be within the mind (internal) or stimulated by external forces as in the high five example.

The final area Royce discussed in this article dealt with interpretation and its temporal capabilities. Royce's theory of "knowledge of the third type" states that "whenever in memory we review our own past, when we reflect upon our own meaning, when we form a plan, or when we ask ourselves what we mean or engage in any inner conversation which forms the commonest of expressions of the activity whereby an individual man attains some sort of explicit knowledge of himself" (Royce 2001, 62), these activities represent interpretation. For him, interpretation not only constituted an internal and external on-going process but also a temporal process. Our human ability to interpret the world around us transcends the immediate present or the notion that I am interpreting signs, symbols, etc. or deal with the present situation.

What he was attempting to illustrate is the notion that interpretation is based upon the past, present, and future. In addition, it can be predicated upon past interpretations. This point is clarified when Royce stated that "when interpretation goes on within the mind of an individual man, it constitutes the very process whereby, as is sometimes said, he 'finds himself,' 'comes to himself,' 'directs himself,' or 'gets his bearings,' especially with reference to time, that is, the present, past, and future" (2001, 64). The triadic model of cognition that Royce presents asserts that humans reflect on interpretation while choosing the temporal state they wish to use to make sense of the interpretations around them.

In conclusion, Royce's 1916 article, "Mind," his last article on the subject of interpretation, represented his final academic writings on the topic of cognition—of a third cognition. He illustrated and highlighted eight key points concerning the nature of cognition: (1) The human process of cognition is not limited to an either/or process, but instead involves a synthesis of perceptual, conceptual, and interpretive knowledge; (2) interpretive knowledge is not an addition to cognitive knowledge; instead it functions as an integral component of both perceptual and conceptual knowledge; (3) interpretive knowledge is both an internal (mind) and external (social) process; (4) interpretation is an ever-present and ongoing process; (5) interpretation is also temporal, based upon past, present, and future interpretations; (6) humans' ability to interpret signs, symbols, and meanings in the past, present, and future allows them to reflect upon interpretations from the past, present, and future; (7) we can interpret not only our own self meanings but the meaning of others; and (8) The process of interpretation happens simultaneously when engaged in a conversation of interpretation, meaning, signs, and symbols.

These eight points represent the major themes and ideas that Royce wrote about in the article "Mind." It is from these concepts and ideas about interpretation and cognition that symbolic interactionists can compare Royce's ideas and concepts to those of the scholars (such as Mead and Blumer) who are currently perceived as the most influential creators and developers of symbolic interactionist thought. The ideas discussed in the next chapter are those that are perceived to be the core, essential concepts for which symbolic interactionist thought is recognized as a critical theoretical perspective in the development of sociology.

CHAPTER VI

THE BASIC IDEAS OF
GEORGE HERBERT MEAD

The focus of this chapter is to investigate the basic ideas of Mead and his social philosophy called social behaviorism. The information representing Mead's basic ideas comes from his posthumously published book, *Mind, Self, and Society* (1934). Instead of attempting to cover all of Mead's basic concepts, the five major ones will be presented here: Mead's conceptualization of social behaviorism; Mead's theory of the mind; the development of Mead's concept of the self; how humans develop within society; and how the notion of community leads to understanding meaning. By exploring these fundamental conceptualizations, an image of Mead's underlying ideas that illustrate portions of his classical symbolic interactionist thought emerge.

Mead's Perspective on Social Behaviorism

In this section, the basic ideas, concepts, and terms that constitute the academic work of Mead will be assessed. I will specifically present the ideas from *Mind, Self, and Society* (1934) that are relevant to the early theory of symbolic interactionism. Though this work was published after Mead's death, the ideas contained therein represent the bulk of his philosophy on the discipline of social behaviorism. Mead's use of the term social behaviorism along with its basic tenets would eventually assist in the formulation of his basic ideas.

The use of Mead's concepts from *Mind, Self, and Society* (1934) in relation to this research is of particular importance to this book for two major reasons: the outline of Mead's social behaviorism represents a systematic overview of early classic symbolic interactionist thought, and this investigation into the basic ideas of Mead will lead us, in the next chapter, to a comparative examination of his conceptualization of symbolic interactionism and the later academic writings of Royce. A comparison of their ideas will mark the second step in asserting that Royce made a significant contribution to the symbolic interactionist theory.

Social Behaviorism

Mind, Self, and Society (1934) starts with an intensive overview of what is meant by the term social behaviorism. Mead arrives at a definition and comprehensive understanding of the concept by investigating social psychology, Watsonian behaviorism, and the philosophy of James.

Traditionally, social psychology focuses on human experience from the point of view of the individual, but Mead prefers a social-psychological approach. More specifically, he allocates a greater significance to communication. This type of social psychological perspective focuses on taking an approach, which puts the individual at the center of their own experience and yet takes into account the social nature of that individual as well.

Social psychology then seeks to explore the dynamics of how the social group helps to determine the perspective of the individual and her/his experience.). Conceptually, Mead's social psychological perspective places a special focus on how an individual self-develops, and how self-consciousness develops from people's experiences. It is from this focus upon the development of the individual self and self-consciousness that he finds a definition of social psychology. Mead therefore identifies the influence of the social group to which the individual belongs to help socially define and construct reality

Not only does Mead create a definition; he also explains the major pursuit of social psychological study. He posits that the physiological mechanism that coincides with individual experience is integral.

This represents the main pursuit of study for those in the social psychology discipline. Notice that the key core concept of social psychology for Mead focuses on the notion that human experience and our own physiological functions are based in the social world. This concept of human experience and bodily functioning, as located within the social structure, remained a major focus for Mead throughout the book, *Mind, Self, and Society* (1934).

The second perspective that Mead presents is pure behaviorism. His discussion of behaviorism is centered on the work of John B. Watson. The behaviorism that Watson discussed can be defined as "an approach to the study of the experience of the individual from the point of view of his conduct, particularly, but not exclusively, the conduct as it is observable by others" (Mead 1967, 2). Watson's behaviorism became a psychological theory; however, it started as a theory focused on animals and animal psychology in the beginning.

During behaviorism's days in animal psychology, introspection was not a concept that could be applied as the animal lacks the ability to convey reasoning of its cognitive process. Hence, there was a greater reliance on external conduct to help determine the extent of consciousness. The inference suggested by introspection was, at the time, very clever; however, it lacked the ability to be empirically studied because it could not be proven using experimentation. This distanced the idea from scientific use and it also proved to be unnecessary in the study of "individual animals" (Mead 1992, 2).

Watson's process of introspection also fell short when considering experiences which are subjective and private. This particular perspective on introspection conforms to the idea that people lack consciousness. Watson's portrayal of the introspective process is explained through the usage of language symbol rather than overt language

Watson's explanation of the introspective process is reductionist, that is, all of human thought can be described in relation to language alone. Mead argued that Watson's explanation of inner experience through external behavior. Hence, it seeks to assess conduct as it occurs, and apply the conduct to explain the experience of the individual. Mead identifies the absence of an observation of an inner experience (or consciousness) as something that is lacking in Watson's approach.

The third perspective that Mead presents in *Mind, Self, and Society* (1934) is that of the American pragmatist William James. Mead began his discussion of James by investigating his 1904 article titled, "Does 'Consciousness' Exist?" In this article, James gives the reader an interesting example of a person in a room surrounded by objects from which two potential standpoints are available. First, there is the standpoint of the "furniture, which, maybe considered from the standpoint of the person who bought it and used it" (Mead 1992, 4). The second standpoint is "from the point of view of its (furniture) color values which attach to it in the minds of the persons who observe them, its aesthetic value, its economic value, its traditional value" (Mead 1992, 4).

These two distinct standpoints can be considered in terms of psychology; that is, they can be viewed in relation to the experiences of the individual. In the case of James's furniture example, "one man puts one value upon it and another gives it another value. But the same objects can be regarded as physical parts of a physical room" (Mead 1992, 4). With this statement, James is "insisting that the two cases differ only in arrangement of certain contents in different series" (Mead 1992, 4). Mead describes this as a process influenced by individuals' perspectives and experiences; each individual that comes in brings with her/him their own points of view from their own experiences which influence their interpretation and context of what is being observed (in this case, the furniture, the walls, the house, etc. This example, though every day in nature, does present a major point in terms of human consciousness. James's example is a statement about human consciousness; that is, the room is not just a historical series, but it also represents the experience of each individual.

The end of Mead's discussion concludes with a brief assessment of the limitations of behaviorism and individual psychology. For Mead, psychology cannot only encompass consciousness alone but expand to a broader context. Given that psychology is a science that uses introspection as an important cognitive process and the individual uses this process more so than other sciences, the individual thus has experiential access. Mead attempts to separate the field of psychology from the basic tenets of social psychology.

Next, Mead focuses his discussion on people's internal or "inner experiences" from a behaviorist perspective. According to Mead, "what one must insist upon is that objectively observable behavior finds expression within the individual, not in the sense of being in another world, a subjective world, but in the sense of being within his organism. Something of this behavior appears in what we term 'attitudes,' the beginnings of acts"…These "attitudes" "give rise to all sorts of responses" (Mead 1992, 5). Mead gives an example of this in the context of a telescope. What is important is not necessarily the instrument (telescope) but rather *how* the astronomer approaches the instrument under certain conditions. Hence, the external act which is observable is tangible, but it does not serve as void of what occurred prior to the act; that is, the context of the relationship between the astronomer and the instrument, or the internal and external processes. The instrument itself is an object, but what the individual does with the instrument gives it purpose, or meaning (Mead 1992:5).

In these two types of behaviorism, it is being said that there are versions which recognize that objects (things) have characteristics and that there are experiences that individuals can have that are considered as happening in an act. According to Mead, the problem with behaviorism, as practiced by Watson, is that it neglects the internal process that is less observable, but yet crucial to the meaning of the act. Speech can be a cue in understanding the internal processes and intrinsic attitudes which might not otherwise be identifiable (Mead 1992: 6).

Hence, a key component that is often underrepresented is the facet of language. Social behaviorists approach language from the context of inner meanings to be expressed through signals and gestures, and as a result, meaning can be revealed (Mead 1992:6). This change in behavioristic perspective allows behaviorism to move from a *psychological* focus to a *social behavioristic* one.

The combination of the elements of behaviorism and James's philosophy of consciousness allows for the formation of social psychology. Social psychology can be defined as "studying the activity or behavior of the individual as it lies within the social process; the behavior of an individual can be understood only in terms of the behavior of the whole social group of which he is a member, since his individual acts are involved in larger, social acts which go beyond himself and which implicate the other members of that group" (Mead 1992, 6–7).

Mead argues that individuals assess the behavior of other individuals within a group. For social psychology, the broader context of society (the whole) precedes the individual (the part) in terms of its influence. Therefore, the individual (the part) is less likely to influence the broader society (the whole). The part is explained in terms of the whole; the whole is not explained in terms of the part(s). The social act is seen as a complex process (Mead 1992:7).

A unique perspective is being offered by Mead's conceptualization of social psychology in that the social process can be understood from the inside as well as the outside. What is tangible is observable activity (e.g., social phenomena, social processes, and social acts) which can be measured and assessed scientifically (Mead 1992:7). This perspective is not a behavioristic one in the sense that it ignores individual's inner experiences. Rather, it assesses the internal experience within the process as a whole. Social behaviorism places emphasis on the parts of the act which are not externally observable. In this vein, Mead has a more solidified perspective than previous attempts of defining and creating the major tenets of social psychology and social behaviorism. In the next section of this chapter, the basic tenets and ideas that further the explanation, definition, and discussion of Mead's social behaviorism and conceptualization of symbolic interactionism are discussed.

Mead and the Mind

Mead saw language as part of, and a crucial component of human social behavior. Not only is language based upon speaking, but Mead asserted that it utilizes varied signs or symbols which help identify inner meanings that might otherwise not be observable (Mead 1992: 13-14Through the use of language, humans are deriving and interpreting meaning from other people even though they may not be consciously aware of it; however, this does not mean that there are no clues of this activity taking place. According to Mead, purpose is identifiable through gestures, symbols, and even non-verbal acts which can be but not necessarily in concert with verbal communication. Hence, it allows for meaning to be derived from overt language, or overt gestures or actions, or a combination of both. Each or collectively, provide insight into the internal dynamics of individual process (meaning, interpretation, perception) (Mead 1992:14

Hence, for Mead, verbal communication is *tangible* insofar as the individual expresses her/his perceptions and meanings with the usage of words, whereas gestures are forms of meanings which cannot be translated into articulate speech (Mead 1992:14). An example of this would be two angry dogs approaching one another. Both dogs may bark, growl, and position themselves to bite or engage in conflict with the intent to harm each other. Even though neither dog spoke, both were able to understand the behavior and actions taking place. In the context of this example, the howling, growling, positioning, and readiness to attack from both dogs can be viewed as a sort of conversation between both animals. Though neither animal speaks its intent, one dog can anticipate the move of the other dog by responding to the last movement or the way in which each dog acts turns into a stimulus for the other dog to respond.

Mead (1992: 43) argues that there is a relationship between these two things. Specifically, the act of one dog is responded to by the other dog, which may prompt *change*. One act may influence the other party to adjust their attitude and their response. While one dog is doing this, the other dog is responding in the same manner by adjusting his relative position or getting ready to change his attitude as well. This set of acts and responses is an example of what Mead calls "a conversation of gestures" (Mead 1992, 43).

Another example of Mead's conversation of gestures is illustrated in the sports of boxing and fencing where one party initiates an action which prompts a response from the other. Action causes reaction, which can include the reactor changing response (e.g., defensive move to offensive attack) which can in turn influence a response from the other party. This example is similar to the angry dogs because, in order to realize success, the individual must consider a significant range of defending and attacking. The individual adjusts to the attitude of the other individual

In the aforementioned case, certain parts of the act serve as a stimulus, or influence, to the other form to adjust to the responses. The response then prompts the next move. There are a series of attitudes and movements that are initiated at the beginning of acts and continue as a process. According to Mead, "the term 'gesture' may be identified with these beginnings of social acts which are stimuli for the response of other forms" (Mead 1992, 43). This is the case with both the angry dog example and the boxing/parrying example. In either case, both angry dogs and fighters are changing their responses to one another, which in turn, forces the other dog or fighter to respond accordingly.

This is a process that is constantly in motion. It includes an interplay of gestures that influence responses, and the responses serving as stimuli for readjustment, until the process exhausts itself. Mead gives us another example in the response of a parent to a crying infant. When an infant cries, it stimulates a response from the parent to react to the crying at hand. The parent's reaction is to respond and then the infant responds to the parent's attempt to acknowledge and assist with the reason the infant is crying. In this example, there is a social process where emotions serve as a mechanism to prompt actions from both actors. The gesture, invoked through emotion, initiate a series of actions which are woven into an interplay of process. Moreover, the expression of meaning or ideas is identified through such actions.

This social process involving gestures changes when the individual responds with an idea in mind. Mead (1992: 45) provides an example of this when he discusses someone shaking their fist in your face. In this example, the shaking of a fist in your face by someone else connotes that not only does that person have a hostile or angry attitude but that they have some sort of idea behind why they feel this way

Mead (1992: 45) accounts for the process of meaning being attainable through gestures, which in turn lead to symbols. In the example of the angry dogs, both dogs were gesturing to each other, which called out a response from both animals as they decided how to act and react. In the case of the shaking the fist example, the shaking fist is a symbol which elicits *meaning*. That is, we have a symbol that both individuals understand based on their previous experience. Mead (1992: 46) argues that the gesture at this point can lead to the more tangible element of language: a symbol that clearly identifies a certain meaning.

The purpose of the gesture is to allow individuals the possibility of adjusting and readjusting to any social act and social situation they find themselves within. (Mead 1992, 46). Adjustment and readjustment within the individual allows for a heightened awareness of acute meaning of not only the individual's attitude, but others' attitudes who are participating with the individual in the given social act. This then enables the individual to adjust her/his subsequent behavior to theirs. This interplay or process is meaningful, and operates on a continuum.

The Social Component of Gestures

According to Mead, individuals initiate gestures to others to get an anticipated response. The other individual is cognizant of the meaning of the gesture because it is understood by her/his own experience. Human meaning appears within our own experience and gestures as long as an individual is able to take the attitude of the person making the gesture and is able to respond to it internally the same way the other person responds externally. Meaning derived from these gestures amounts to significant symbols whether external (between different individuals) or internal (between a given individual and himself)" (Mead 1992, 47).

In this sense, the consciousness of an individual, and the process of ebb and flow involved in deriving meaning, is dependent on our ability to take the attitude of others toward their own gestures. Mead's philosophy of social behaviorism is grounded in gestures serving as significant symbols. It is only through this process that one can understand and appreciate the existence of mind and intelligence.

The essence of thought then involves the internalization of our experience(s) to the external gestures of others. That is, the internalization of gestures leads to the creation of significant symbols because they have shared meaning for all societal members. If individuals did not have the ability to arouse certain attitudes or responses from other individuals, then they could not internalize significant symbols nor be aware of their meanings This ever-present human process contributes to consciousness, which includes the taking of the attitude of the other toward one's self, or towards one's own behavior "is responsible for the genesis of and existence of mind or consciousness—namely, the taking of the attitude of the other toward one's self, or towards one's own behavior" (Mead 1992, 48).

Mead's Gesture Versus Wundt's Gesture

Mead's socially orientated perspective on gestures differs greatly from the early twentieth-century psychologist Wundt. Mead charges that Wundt's parallelism can only be attributed to talking alone, rather than more complex social processes such as conflict. It is argued that Wundt sees gestures of one individual as prompting the same emotional attitude and the same idea as who initiated it. This cannot be attributed to most other forms of social processes.

Wundt's conversation of gestures is previously described as not involving significant symbols or gestures. In this sense, from the angry dog example, the dogs are not engaging in language/conversation, and there is an absence of ideas in the minds of the dogs. Humans have a more sophisticated framework to operate under. Here, language is used to convey meaning, and if this gesture is understood, it calls out an idea, making it a significant gesture.

For Mead, Wundt's perspective on gestures and parallelism is problematic. For example, if an individual shakes his fist in your face, the act is a gesture that invokes a reaction. However the response may vary (e.g., prompting a verbal confrontation, a physical altercation, or the other party to leave without engaging in any confrontation).

In Mead's example, no matter what response a person decides to act upon, there is the possibility of different responses. This is not true in the case of Wundt's theory of gestures, which restricts the process to be an exact or parallel response to the gesture. For Mead, Wundt's concept of the gesture focuses not just on individuals and what they may be thinking about, but it also involves the concept of emotion; whereas Mead's concept of the gesture involves the responses to the acts of each individual as long as there is a stimulus to react to in the environment. By comparison, Mead's version of gestures differs from Wundt's psychical state in that it emphasizes the process of thinking about the thoughts that the other individual is thinking along with an individual's emotional state. There is no guarantee in Wundt's case that one individual's gesture will arouse the intended response from another individual.

This quotation, in reference to Wundt, causes Mead to posit the following question: "How, in terms of Wundt's psychological analysis of communication, does a responding organism get or experience the same idea or psychical correlate of any given gesture that the organism making this gesture has" (Mead 1992, 49)? Mead's answer to this question addresses the major underlying problem of Wundt's theory of gestures. That is, Wundt's theory presents 'selves' as an antecedent to the social process. In this vein, communication is best explained within that process. It is argued that individuals must enter into meaningful relation within the social process *before* communication.

Mead explains the social aspect and social process involved in communication as important. He forwards that the body is not a self in and of itself; rather, it becomes one when the mind has developed in the context of understanding social reality and social experience. If we take Wundt's perspective, then an individual has a mind from the very beginning, which makes and explains an individual's social process within which experiences happen. If that is indeed the case, then Wundt's explanation of this process would make for a murky explanation in that it could not explain the development of a mind, nor could it explain the interaction between minds.

However, from the perspective of Mead, the human mind is developed and maximizes potential through the process of communication. This communication arises through a conversation of gestures in a social process.

Mead and Defining Meaning

Thus far, Mead has been concerned with how humans communicate and use gestures to adjust to one another's responses and act with other humans. Through the use of gestures, significant gestures, and significant symbols, humans are able to call out responses and anticipate the acts of one another and then, in turn, adjust to one another in a conversation of gestures. These adjustments that take place within the conversation of gestures between humans have meaning. Mead contends that adjustment is contingent on meaning.

The concept of "meaning" that Mead describes comes about through the relation between the gesture of one individual and the subsequent reaction from another individual. An alternative way to think of this concept would be to examine the relationship between a stimulus (as a gesture) and the later phases of the social act; this helps contribute to how 'meaning' originates and exists" (Mead 1992, 76). From this perspective, meaning arises from something objectively there as a relation between certain phases of the social act.

Mead explains the development of meaning as a threefold relationship between parties where a gesture by one individual elicits a response from a second, and gestures are conveyed to subsequent phases of the given social act. Meaning arises in the context of the interplay of gestures, responses and subsequent action(s).

In the example, "the gesture stands for a certain resultant of the social act, a resultant to which there is a definite response on the part of the individual involved therein; so that meaning is given or stated in terms of response" (Mead 1992, 76). This development of meaning occurs in the human social process through symbols or the process of symbolization. A practical example of this process is illustrated in Mead's baby chick situation. A baby chick responds to the cluck of the hen because the noise (cluck) has meaning to it (e.g., availability of food). This example can be applied to the human situation by changing the chick to a human baby and the mother hen to a human mother. In either case, the result is the same; the human baby or chick responds to the meaning of the crying or the cluck.

Mead further defines meaning by stating that "the social process, as involving communication, is in a sense responsible for the appearance of new objects in the field of experience of the individual organisms implicated in that process" (Mead 1992, 77). Without people creating objects for others to respond to, there would be no meaning to derive because there would be no objects from which to create. This statement addresses two concepts. The first is that objects, in relation to meaning, are important because of their ability to draw out responses. The second is that the meaning of objects plays a function in our social experience and the social process.

However, there is a third component to Mead's concept of meaning and objects. "The social process in a sense constitutes the objects to which it responds, or to which it is an adjustment" (Mead 1992, 77). Mead elaborates this further by saying that objects are related to in the context of meanings that are ascribed to them given individuals' experiences. Depending on how others react, adjustments are made in the process of a conversation of gestures (in the early stages) and then language (in the later stages).

In Mead's version of this process, "awareness and consciousness are not necessary to the presence of meaning in the process of social experience" (Mead 1992, 77). This is possible because gestures on the part of one of the social actors influences a response by the other social actor, and adjustments are subsequently made depending on the response of the other. Mead therefore posits that this interplay emerges as a process, and the emergence of consciousness or awareness of meaning follows afterward

Symbolization refers to the process whereby objects are ascribed meaning. These objects would not exist except without the context of social relationships and the exchange of action of social process where symbolization occurs. Mead argues that language is a mechanism whereby symbolization is conveyed and understood, but it is important to note that meaning is ascribed or created through language. This especially applies to the social process as it relates to the interplay of individuals who are constantly adjusting and re-adjusting. As such, there is a rise and existence of new objects in the social process, objects which Mead argues are dependent upon or constituted by these meanings This especially applies to the "social process as it relates the responses of one individual to the gestures of another, as the meanings of the latter, and is thus responsible for the rise and existence of new objects in the social situation, objects dependent upon or constituted by these meanings" (Mead 1992, 78).

Mead suggests that meaning is not constituted outside of experience, but rather within the social process of experience (the individual adjusting and re-adjusting with others. This suggests that it is more internal, or on a micro level, rather than an external, or macro level. Meaning is influenced by the individual's experience, both with others in the broader social group. Overall, this means that "the responses of one organism to the gesture of another in any given social act is the meaning of that gesture, and also is in a sense responsible for the appearance or coming into being of the new object—or the content of an old object—which that gesture refers through the outcome of the given social act in which it is an early phase" (Mead 1992, 78).

Mead (1992: 78) applies this concept to the object by explaining that objects are made tangible to the human psyche through the process of social experience, specifically through communication and adjustment of behavior among individuals. However, the interpretation of gestures, although taking part in the internal dynamics of the mind, are argued to be influenced greatly through an external context (insofar as it involves an overt, physical and a physiological process of social experience)

Of note is that Mead believes that while meaning can be described in terms of language (as the highest and most complex stage of development), it only extracts out of the social process what exists there already. Hence, it facilitates meaning, but does not in and of itself, create meaning.

In sum, two major points are being made by Mead to explain social process. First, communication allows for the appearance of a new set of objects in nature which exist in relation to it (objects). Second, the gesture of an individual and the adjusted response of the other to that gesture helps to provide meaning. Both of these things are basic and complementary logical aspects of social process. For Mead, the structure of 'meaning' involves a triadic model between gesture, adjustive response, and the resultant of the social act which the gesture initiates. The existence of meaning is dependent on how the adjustive responses of the second party are directed toward the re-gesture of the first.

Mead contends that the essence of meaning can be found within social experience, or in relation to it. One manner in which objects assume meaning is in the context of their relation to an individual or individuals. This differs from Wundt's version of meaning that he viewed as principally within a psychical content. Instead, Mead posits that meaning becomes conscious only when it becomes identified or in correlation to significant symbols. The symbols serve as a physical component that are attributed meaning to that individual. In other words, the object has no meaning in and of itself, but it is ascribed meaning because the individual ascribes purpose to that object.

Mead and the Self

As indicated earlier through the discussion of Mead's work, language is one of the most important concepts to consider in the development of the human mind and intelligence. However, the same is true in the development of the human self. Mead cites the importance of the language to the development of self (Mead 1992, 135). This perspective on the human self is unique, because it conceptualizes the human self as developing out of a process. Mead emphasizes this idea by explaining that the self is indeed a process, or development. It is not something that we are born with but rather a systematic process which involves social experience(s).

Though our human self-arises out of a social experience and social environment, the majority of our intelligence requires no self. According to Mead, human experiences can occur without the self; however, Mead warns us that "one must, of course, under those conditions, distinguish between the experience that immediately takes place and our own organization of it into the experience of the self. One says upon analysis that a certain item had its place in his experience, in the experience of his self" (Mead 1992, 135). Mead elaborates on this statement when he states that "we do inevitably tend at a certain level of sophistication to organize all experience into that of a self" (Mead 1992, 135).

An example of this can be found in our human psyche which can comprehend, appreciate and ascribe meaning to emotions such as pain or pleasure without experiencing a new experience. In other words, what has been experienced in the past is enough to appreciate the emotive value, or feeling, that is constituted to the. Another example can be seen when memories are based upon their correlation to self. Past experiences serve as the timeline in general whereas the specific dates and times may not be as cogent. When looking at a picture, the individual tens to place the context to her/his past experience because that provides the context of meaning to that individual.

Before moving on with Mead's discussion of the self, a distinction must be made between the self and the body. Mead contends that the body can be present and engage in an advanced manner although potentially absent of self-involvement being part of the process. He argues that parts of the body can be lost without any significant impact on the self. He suggests that it can be compared to a table, where the table represents itself. As such, Mead makes the case that the body does not experience itself as a whole, but rather that the self is in fact an object to itself (Mead 1992:136).

The word 'self' is in fact reflexive, insofar as it can be both subject and object. The term suggests that it is an experience with, or an experience of, one's self Mead was cognizant of the fact that other theories of the 'self' operated under basic premises that consciousness in some manner made possible for an object being an object to itself. However, his task was to underscore that in giving emphasis to consciousness, it is necessary to look for some form of experience for the individual to be able to become an object to itself In other theories of the self, "it was assumed that consciousness in some way carried this capacity of an object being an object to itself" (Mead 1992, 137).

Mead finds a solution to this problem in the example of an individual who may be running to escape another who may be pursuing her/him. In this context, the person running away is entirely focused on that action, and in doing so has no consciousness of self during this time. This represents an example of where the self does not enter, or is absent from the body.

In this example, there is a contrast between an experience where the self as an object does not enter, and an experience of memory and imagination in which the self is the core object in the equation The point Mead is making with this example is that "the self is entirely disguisable from an organism that is surrounded by things and acts with reference to things, including parts of its own body. These latter may be objects like other objects, but they are just objects out there in the field, and they do not involve a self that is an object to the organism" (Mead 1992, 137). This point, according to Mead, is "frequently overlooked" (Mead 1992, 137).

The Question of Self as an Object

There's a question that Mead must solve in relation to the self as an object. He questions how an individual can get outside of her/himself in a manner that would have the individual become an object to her/himself. Indeed, Mead argues that reason would not be complete unless it was immersed in the field of experience. Alternatively, the individual could also enter into the experimental field as others with whom she/he acts in social contexts (Mead 1992: 138). Mead charges that reason cannot become so objectified. In this case, "reason cannot become impersonal unless it takes an objective, non- affective attitude toward itself; otherwise, we have just consciousness, not self-consciousness" (Mead 1992, 138). Also, "it is necessary to rational conduct that the individual should thus take an objective, impersonal attitude toward himself, that he should become an object to himself" (Mead 1992, 138). This means that "the individual organism is obviously an essential and important fact or constituent element of the empirical situation in which it acts; and without taking objective account of itself as such, it cannot act intelligently, or rationally" (Mead 1992, 138).

For Mead (1992: 138), the individual experiences her/himself through the perspectives of other members of the broader social group. The individual thus becomes, or assumes the role of an object insofar as others view her/him in a certain manner, and the individual is cognizant of such, and can internalize that projection. Whether or not the individual accepts that 'judgment' is not as important to the process as having the understanding of how she/he is being perceived by others. In this vein, the self becomes objectified. Mead suggests that the concept of communication is important insofar as it provides a form of behavior in which the organism may become an object to her/himself.

With regard to communication, that is needed for the introduction of 'self' (Mead 1992:138-139). Mead gives emphasis to the individual as using communication to engage in experiences with others, including their interpretation of them. At the same time, the individual engages in a cognitive process which would be similar to communicating to others, except now the individual assesses her/his own conduct through her/his own experiences. Here, the individual not only hears her/himself but she/he responds to one's self, and engages in communicating to one's self as they would do so to others, except now the individual replies to her/himself. It is in this process that the individual becomes an object to her/himself

The Self as a Social Self

According to Mead, "the self, as that which can be an object to itself, is essentially a social structure, and it arises in social experience" (Mead 1992, 140). Though, "after a self has arisen, it in a certain sense provides for itself its social experiences, and so we can conceive of an absolutely solitary self" (Mead 1992, 149). However, "it is impossible to conceive a self-arising outside of social experience" (Mead 1992, 140). This is true for Mead because "when the self has arisen, we can think of a person in solitary confinement for the rest of his life, but who still has himself as a companion, and is able to think and to converse with himself as he had communicated with others" (Mead 1992, 140).

"This process to which I [Mead] just referred, of responding to one's self as another responds to it, taking part in one's own conversation with others, being aware of what one is saying and using that awareness of what one is saying to determine what one is going to say there after—that is a process which we are all familiar" (Mead 1992, 140). Within this process, humans "are continually following up our own address to other persons by an understanding of what we are saying, and using that understanding in the direction of our continued speech" (Mead 1992, 140). In addition, "we are also finding out what we are going to say, what we are going to do, by saying and doing, and in the process, we are continually controlling the process itself" (Mead 1992, 140).

If this process is thought of in terms of the aforementioned conversation of gestures, readers can see that "what we say calls out a certain response in another and that in turn changes our own action, so that we shift from what we started to do because of the reply the other makes" (Mead 1992, 141). In this sense, "the conversation of gestures is the beginning of communication. The individual comes to carry on a conversation of gestures with himself. He says something and that calls out a certain reply in himself which makes him change what he was going to say" (Mead 1992, 141). In turn, "one starts to say something, we will presume an unpleasant something, but when he starts to say it, he realizes it is cruel" (Mead 1992, 141). Mead illustrates this process of the self as a social process in the following example:

> The effect on himself of what he is saying checks him; there is here a conversation of gestures between the individual and himself. We mean by significant speech that the action is one that affects the individual himself, and that the effect upon the individual himself is others. Now we, so to speak, amputate that social phase and dispense with it for the time being, so that one is talking to one's self as one would talk to another person (Mead 1992, 141).

Within this social process of the self, the process of abstraction (internal dynamics or what occurs within the individual's mental process) becomes the primary stage of the act. Specifically, one thinks to act first, making this action dependent on the act commission of the act. Hence, the internal dynamics remain an important part of a social process that operates on a continuum (Mead 1992, 141). This means, according to Mead, that the important process of thinking is, in fact, an internal conversation that is occurring Mead provides an example to illustrate. The individual is able to separate the significance of what she/he is about to say and prepares for it prior to its communicated form.

The idea that a human responds to himself "is necessary to the self, and it is this sort of social conduct which provides behavior within which the self appears" (Mead 1992, 142). For Mead, "there is no other form of behavior than the linguistic in which the individual is an object to himself, and, so far as I can see, the individual is not a self in the reflexive sense unless he is an object to himself." This underlying concept places a high emphasis on "communication, since this is a type of behavior in which the individual does so respond to himself" (Mead 1992, 142).

This fundamental belief leads Mead to proclaim that "what determines the amount of the self that gets into communication is the social experience itself" (Mead 1992, 142). Examples of this can be found, for instance, when people have relations with others on a daily basis. Each individual conversation with each person yields a different set of responses, acts, and reactions, yet more importantly, each encounter with every individual illustrates Mead's point that "there are all sorts of different selves answering to all sorts of different social reactions" (Mead 1992, 142). Thus, "it is the social process itself that is responsible for the appearance of the self; it is not there as a self apart from this type of experience" (Mead 1992, 142).

Generalized Other

In this section, Mead's conceptualization of the generalized other is discussed. According to Mead, "the organized community or social group which gives to the individual his unity of self may be called 'the generalized other'" (1992, 154). Not only does the social group give the self its unity but also "the attitude of the generalized other is the attitude of the whole community" (Mead 1992, 154). An example of the generalized other can be seen "in the case of such a social group as a ball team, the team is the generalized other in so far as it enters—as an organized or social activity—in the experience of any one of the individual members of it" (Mead 1992, 154).

Though, if a human is "to develop a self in the fullest sense, it is not sufficient for him merely to take the attitudes of other human individuals toward himself and toward one another within the human social process, and to bring that social process as a whole into his individual experience merely in these terms" (Mead 1992, 154). An individual "must also, in the same way that he takes the attitudes of other individuals toward himself and toward one another, take their attitudes toward the various phases or aspects of the common social activity or set of social undertakings in which, as members of an organized society or social group, they are all engaged" (Mead 1992, 154–155). If a person generalizes "these individual attitudes of that organized society or social group itself, as a whole, act toward different social projects which at any given time it is carrying out, or toward the various larger phases of the general social process which constitutes its life and of which these projects are specific manifestations" (Mead 1992, 155).

The social process and social formation of the generalized other is "the essential basis and prerequisite of the fullest development of that individual's self" (Mead 1992, 155). However, this is "only in so far as he takes the attitudes of the organized social group to which he belongs toward the organized, cooperative social activity or set of such activities in which the group as such is engaged, does he develop a complete self or possess the sort of complete self he has developed" (Mead 1992, 155). Though, "on the other hand, the complex cooperative processes and activities and institutional functions of organized human society are also possible only in so far as every individual involved in them or belonging to that society can take the general attitudes of all other such individuals with reference to these processes and institutional functioning" (Mead 1992, 155).

The basic ideas of Mead presented in this chapter were meant to present some of the fundamental philosophical ideas of the social philosopher whose academic works influenced symbolic interactionist thought. While the concepts presented are in no way shape or form exhaustive, they were meant to establish a basic framework from which to work. In the next section, the focus will be on taking this basic framework and some of its concepts and compare and contrast the similarities and differences between them and those of Royce. This will be the first step toward investigating whether and to what degree Royce made a contribution to symbolic interactionist thought.

CHAPTER VII

COMPARING THE BASIC IDEAS

OF ROYCE AND MEAD

The purpose of this chapter is to examine the basic ideas of George Herbert Mead and the ideas presented in later academic works of Josiah Royce. By examining Royce's later writings and Mead's basic concepts, a crucial link between the two is established: Royce made a significant contribution to the development of early symbolic interactionism.

Mead and Royce on Language and Meaning

For Mead, language is not separate but a prominent part of social behavior. Not only is language based upon speaking, but it includes non-verbal cues and symbols which convey meaning. Through the use of language, humans are deriving and interpreting meaning from other people, even though they may not be consciously aware of it; however, this does not mean that there are no clues of this activity taking place. As such, purpose is conveyed through actions with or without language (e.g., variations of eye contact, or body positioning or movements) which lead to the response of the other social actor

While Royce does not specifically discuss the term language or its overall meaning, he does suggest that humans are actively involved in understanding and deriving meaning from signs and symbols. Royce illustrates this point in *The Problem of Christianity* (1913). Here, he describes the situation of a traveler at a signpost. Royce suggests that humans understand a signpost is by reading it. In this vein, the sign-post serves as a guide, but it needs interpretation to allow for it to assist the individual in showing the way

The signpost that Royce discusses is "constituted of at least three distinct minds" (Royce 1968, 347). The first distinct mind is the intent of having the directions potentially conveyed to others is through the physical construction of the sign- The second distinct mind is the necessity of understanding language to be able to understand the meaning of such The third mind is the process of interpretation, where individual goes beyond reading it and engages in a process of understanding how to apply such directions.

He takes this example one step further when he considers the "three distinct mental functions" or "three minds" involved in interpreting the sign-post (Royce 1968, 347). First is "the function of the mind whose purpose the sign expresses" (Royce 1968, 347). Second, "there is the mind which is guided by the interpretation of the sign" (Royce 1968, 347). Lastly, there "is the function of the interpreter to whom the reading of the sign is due" (Royce 1968, 347).

Note: This paragraph is repetitive saying the same thing as what preceded it. Unless you are okay with it, consider deleting it.

The example of the signpost and the complex process of interpreting the meaning of the signpost illustrates the point that Mead was trying to make about humans constantly being engaged in the interpretation of language (signs, symbols) in their daily lives. This example also illustrates a clear image of a sign that anyone could see or interpret on any given day. Moreover, by interpreting the meaning of the sign-post based upon the "three minds" and "three mental functions," a person is able to derive the meaning of not only the context of the situation but also the sign itself. According to Royce then, humans act upon the interpretation of a sign and its meaning(s). In the case of the signpost, a person would interpret the sign and its meaning externally and then act accordingly.

A second example of how people interpret meaning from language (signs, symbols, gestures, etc.) comes from an internal example. In *The Problem of Christianity* (1913), Royce discusses the meaning of facial expressions (gestures) in relation to one's neighbors. Royce places importance in reading how others express themselves through facial expressions, and the meaning such expressions convey. He also cites how others can read one's own facial expressions without any emphasis on language However, this does not suggest that a person cannot look at his or her face in the mirror and indirectly perceive his or her facial expressions. Since a person cannot merely rely on the facial expressions observed in the mirror and his or her own information, they have to interpret the signs of others.

Royce places due emphasis on the importance of others evaluating us. At the very least, we are able to learn how our expressive movements appear through the report of others. This affords social actors to view ourselves through the 'eyes' or perspective of others, and fills in notable 'gaps' insofar as our own interpretations alone are limited in scope and bias. External assessments provide a secondary, if not a more objective viewpoint that may help the individual understand how her/his expressive movements convey meaning(s). The example of interpreting our facial expressions illustrates the idea that people derive meaning from signs, symbols, gestures, etc. on both an external and internal level. The process of interpretation that Royce discusses in relation to our facial expressions illustrates two points: First, people possess the ability to interpret, and hence, assist in understanding the meaning or meanings of their neighbors, and second, understanding or deriving of meaning from the interpretation of our neighbors' reactions (in this case facial expressions) can assist in creating "self" meaning and understanding.

These two points illustrate that Royce's philosophy on the "process of interpretation" involves a synthesis of both internal and external meaning. It also illustrates that Royce's process of interpretation is vitally important to understanding ourselves and others, and creates a social philosophy that makes meaning important in its own right. It is especially true in relation to Mead's conception of language and meaning, because deriving and understanding meaning is an ongoing and infinite process that involves both internal and external sources of understanding meaning in language. The very component of Mead's ideas on deriving meaning through language can also be found within Royce's later academic works. Thus, interpreting the signs, symbols, or in Mead's terminology— gestures—is a vital component of Royce's social philosophy.

Royce and Mead on Defining Meaning

The concept of "meaning" that Mead describes operates within the social process of gesture of an individual and the subsequent behavior by another individual who reacts to that gesture. The gesture is accorded 'meaning' depending on the behavior of the responding

The relationship between a gesture and the later stage of the social act are tantamount to formulating meaning. The gesture serves as the stimulus to the act but it is in the primus stage of gesture that meaning is created, and influences future action and meaning(s). Mead accounts that the gesture of one organism, the response of another organism, and gesture to subsequent phases of the social act constitute a threefold relationship, or a matrix which develops an expansive and encompassing meaning.

From Mead's perspective, the concept of meaning "is thus not to be conceived, fundamentally, as a state of consciousness, or as a set of organized relations existing or subsisting mentally outside the field of experience into which they enter; on the contrary, it should be conceived objectively, as having its existence entirely within this field itself" (Mead 1992, 78). Overall, this means that "the responses of one organism to the gesture of another in any given social act is the meaning of that gesture, and also is in a sense responsible for the appearance or coming into being of the new object—or the content of an old object—to which that gesture refers through the outcome of the given social act in which it is an early phase" (Mead 1992, 78).

The best example of people acting on and deriving meaning in a social context comes from an internal example provided by Royce in *The Problem of Christianity* (1913) where he discussed the meaning of facial As described in an earlier example, this statement does not necessarily suggest that a person cannot look and indirectly perceive their face in the mirror, nor does it mean that people cannot see and interpret our own facial expressions. Since we cannot rely upon the facial expressions observed in the mirror alone, we have to interpret the signs of others.

This example of interpreting our facial expressions is "typical for the way in which we interpret the usual signs of his mind which our neighbor gives to us" (Royce 1968, 359). This is true for Royce, who says, "I never normally view my own organism in a perspective which is closely analogous to the perspective in which I constantly perceive the body and the movements of my fellow man" (Royce 1968, 359). Overall, since we cannot conceive of our selves through our own internal interpretations alone, insight into one's own expressive movements is gained through secondary observation; others judge us, and assume greater influence insofar as identity formation. More specifically, individuals learn how their own expressive movements appear through the report of others.

In addition, this example of interpreting our facial expressions is similar to Mead's discussion of deriving meaning from gestures. Mead makes this point when he states that adjustments take place through communication (from gestures) in less advanced societies and from significant symbols on the higher levels of human evolution.

Whether humans are exchanging gestures at the lowest or highest levels is not of concern to Mead because the concept of deriving "meaning" happens in both instances. This is true, according to Mead, because meaning is accorded within the context of gesture and the subsequent behavior of another to that gesture. When another organism engages in resultant behavior, then it is understood as having meaning. Mead's example of gestures having meaning that is translated from one human being to another is very similar to Royce's conceptualization of deriving meaning from facial expressions.

Royce and Mead on the Generalized Other

According to Mead, "the organized community or social group which gives to the individual his unity of self may be called 'the generalized other'" (Mead 1992, 154). Not only does the social group give the self its unity, but also "the attitude of the generalized other is the attitude of the whole community" (Mead 1992, 154). An example of the generalized other can be seen "in the case of such a social group as a ball team, the team is the generalized other in so far as it enters—as an organized or social activity—in the experience of any one of the individual members of it" (Mead 1992, 154).

Though, if a human being is "to develop a self in the fullest sense, it is not sufficient for him merely to take the attitudes of other human individuals toward himself and toward one another within the human social process, and to bring that social process as a whole into his individual experience merely in these terms" (Mead 1992, 154). An individual "must also, in the same way that he takes the attitudes of other individuals toward himself and toward one another, take their attitudes toward the various phases or aspects of the common social activity or set of social undertakings in which, as members of an organized society or social group, they are all engaged" (Mead 1992, 154–155). If a person generalizes "these individual attitudes of that organized society or social group itself, as a whole, act toward different social projects which at any given time is carrying out, or toward the various larger phases of the general social process which constitutes its life and of which these projects are specific manifestations" (Mead 1992, 155).

We can see a clear example of this notion of the "generalized other" in Royce's book *The Problem of Christianity* (1913). For Royce, interpretation and comparison on a larger level reflects a need for a community of interpretation/comparison. Since humans are constantly engaged in the process of interpreting and comparing one another, Royce creates the idea of a "community of interpretation." The community of interpretation is defined below:

> Since the same will to interpret you is also expressive of my analogous interests in all my other neighbors, what I here and now specifically aim to do is this: I mean to interpret you to somebody else, to some other neighbor, who is neither yourself nor myself. Three of us, then, I seek to bring into the desired unity of interpretation (Royce 1968, 314).

This "community of interpretation" is triadic, according to Royce. "If, then, I am worthy to be an interpreter at all, we three—you, my neighbor, whose mind I would fain interpret—you, my kindly listener, to whom I am to address my interpretation—we three constitute a community. Let us give this community a technical name, let us call it a 'community of interpretation'" (Mead 1968, 315). This notion of a "community of interpretation" has far-reaching implications for Royce's social philosophy. In relation to Mead's concept of the "generalized other," Royce's "Community of Interpretation" shares in the notion that there is a shared, or community of, understanding of the world in which one lives. Mead's concept of the "generalized other" illustrates that the shared connections with one's social group or society has an effect on one's responses or actions in relation to one's neighbors or other community members. The same can be said of Royce's "community of interpretation" as he views the process of interpretation as happening within a community or shared experience.

In addition, the actual interpretations and meanings being derived from a person's neighbors are affected by that person's relation to his or her own community. However, although Royce did not view his process of interpretation or deriving of meaning on a societal level, he used the term "community" to represent the actual community in which one resides. This community can vary depending upon the setting in which a person lives. For example, a city, town, or rural township can be considered a community. This in no way implies that these larger social connections were any less relevant than Mead's focus on "society." During Royce's lifetime, American society was based upon communities of people rather than the notion of the United States. Thus, Royce likely saw the larger implications of the process of interpretation on a societal level.

Language and meaning, defining meaning, and the concept of the "generalized other" represent a small but highly representative collection of major and fundamental Meadian ideas. The connections between Mead and Royce are very strong, considering that Royce and his major academic works predate Mead's ideas expressed in *Mind, Self, and Society* (1934). The shared aspects of both social philosophers' academic works illustrate that Royce did indeed make a contribution to symbolic interactionist thought. Royce's link to language, defining meaning, and the "generalized other" are important points to establish because of their essential and vital role in the creation and understanding of symbolic interactionist theory. These similarities should be kept in mind even though the next chapter transitions into an investigation of the basic ideas of Blumer and his synthesized definition of symbolic interactionism.

CHAPTER VIII
HERBERT BLUMER
AND SYMBOLIC INTERACTIONISM

Over the years, sociology has developed a myriad of theories (of various ranges) that assist in the explanation of the social world. Though these social/cultural theories are constantly changing, there are several that have withstood the test of time. These few select theories are studied under the sub-discipline known as classical sociological theory. One such theory, symbolic interactionism, has developed into a mainstay within the discipline and a research perspective of many sociologists and academics around the world.

This chapter investigates and explores the depths of what is meant by symbolic interactionist theory through the work of sociologist Blumer. The main purpose in studying Blumer's definition of symbolic interactionism is of a threefold nature: First, to discuss Royce's contribution beyond classical (Mead-based) symbolic interactionism; second, to investigate the details of Blumer's definition beyond his three basic premises, and third, to justify the use of Blumer's definition of symbolic interactionism.

Defining Symbolic Interactionism

The definition of symbolic interactionism to be investigated comes from Blumer. Blumer originated and coined the term symbolic interactionism accidentally in 1937 when he used the term in the article, "Man and Society" (Blumer 1969, 1). According to Blumer's definition of symbolic interactionism, there are only three major premises:

(1) The first premise is that human beings engage in action based on the meanings that the things have for them (Blumer 1969, 2).

(2) The second premise is that the meaning of such things arises out of the social interaction that one has with others (Blumer 1969, 2).

(3) The third premise is that these meanings are understood and adjusted through an interpretive process (Blumer 1969, 2).

Blumer, in the book, *Symbolic Interactionism: Perspective and Method* (1969), systematically explains and explores each of these premises in detail. The first premise appears to be very straightforward, but Blumer argues that this is largely ignored or downplayed by contemporary social science and psychology. Blumer suggests that this view is given minimal credence because sociologists and psychologists have a tendency to treat human behavior as being influenced by outside factors, rather than their intrinsic internal dynamics as the first premise advances.

Psychologists look for such factors when they conduct research projects that focus on "stimuli, attitudes, conscious or unconscious motives, various kinds of inputs, perception and cognition, and various features of personal organization to account for given forms or instances of human conduct" (Blumer 1969, 3). While psychologists focus on individualized and mental-based factors in their assessments of the ways human beings act in relation to the meanings of things, sociologists focus on different factors. Conversely, sociologists emphasize other outside influences such as social roles, norms and values, social pressures, in-group and out-group dynamics, and the role of disenfranchisement and how it affects behavior The sociological factors used in assessing the way humans act in relation to meaning centers on group and larger cultural factors rather than individual and mental phenomena.

Though both psychology and sociology use different factors (either individualized or cultural) in their assessment of human meaning, neither avoids the problem of being a mere one-way process. Blumer (1969:3) argues that the factors assessed in psychology are limiting because they only focus on identification of initiating factors and the subsequent behavior rather than assessing the meaning behind why individuals act.

Blumer (1969:3) also critiques sociology insofar as the discipline attempts to assess meaning by integrating it in the initiating factors, or by viewing it as a neutral intervening link between the initiating factors and the subsequent behaviors. Both of these social-science perspectives fall into the trap of only assessing *one way* in which to derive *meaning*. In psychology, meaning is merged into causal factors, whereas in sociology, meaning can be ignored while added emphasis is placed on initiating factors. The limiting process of deriving meaning that psychology and sociology suffer can be fixed through the use of symbolic interactionism. According to Blumer, symbolic interactionism fuses together the ideas of psychology and sociology in relation to deriving *meaning*. However, that is not the only premise that establishes symbolic interactionism's unique character.

The second major premise of symbolic interactionism, "refers to the *source* of meaning" that humans are involved in creating (Blumer 1969, 3). For Blumer, there are two ways in which meaning is created. The first way "is to regard meaning as being intrinsic to the thing that has it, as being part of the objective make-up of the thing" (Blumer 1969, 3). This principle can be illustrated by the example that a car is a car, a snowflake is a snowflake, etc. In philosophy, this manner of creating sources of meaning is properly termed "realism" (Blumer 1969, 4).

The second way in which humans create sources of meaning focuses on viewing *meaning* as a *psychical accretion* insofar as the physical thing is accredited meaning by the individual. This psychical accretion is treated as elements of the person's psyche or mind. Examples of elements in this process would include the contexts of feelings, ideas, memories, and motives. More simply put, Blumer advances that the process of the creation of meaning involves the psychological elements that are involved in the process of the perception of the thing. Hence, one seeks to explain the meaning of a thing by focusing on the psychological elements that produce meaning.

Though this particular process of creating meaning served as a model for psychology and other social sciences earlier in their existence; it is not without one major criticism. This criticism is that "by lodging the meanings of things in psychological elements (constituents) this can limit the processes of the formation of meaning to whatever processes are involved in arousing and bringing together the given psychological elements that produce the meaning" (Blumer 1969, 4).

The limiting factors presented in the "realist" and "psychical" explanations of the creation of the sources of meaning led Blumer to explain how symbolic interactionism differs from both. Symbolic interactionism "views meaning as having a different source than those held by the two dominant views considered above" because symbolic interactionism "does not regard meaning as emanating from the intrinsic makeup of the thing that has meaning; nor does it see meaning as arising through a coalescence of psychological elements in the person" (Blumer 1969, 4). Instead of symbolic interactionism becoming trapped in an either/or situation like the "realism" and "psychical" elements, it takes on a middle of the road approach.

The symbolic interactionist perspective accords meaning as resulting from the process of human. This means that symbolic interactionists view meaning as contingent upon how others act toward the person. This also means that for symbolic interactionism, meaning is considered to be socially constructed through defining the interlocking processes of interaction among. This places symbolic interactionism in a unique perspective because it has larger implications on the perspective as a whole.

With regard to the third major premise that Blumer advances many incorrectly perceive that "the meaning of things is formed in the context of social interaction and is delivered by the person from that interaction. Meaning created by a person is not merely an application of the meaning at hand because this perspective fails to appreciate the usage of meanings by the individual in her/his action involves a specific process of interpretation.

The idea of an "interpretive process" is a major underlying premise of the symbolic interactionist perspective. This process of interpretation can be defined as having two essential parts. First, "the actor indicates to himself the things toward which he is acting; he has to point that out to himself the things that have meaning" (Blumer 1969, 5). The creation of such indicators rests in "an internalized social process in that the actor is interacting with himself. This interaction with himself is something other than an interplay of psychological elements; it is an instance of the person engaging in a process of communication with himself" (Blumer 1969, 5).

The second essential part of the process of interpretation involves the notion that "interpretation becomes a matter of handling meanings" (Blumer 1969, 5). That is to say, "the actor selects, checks, suspends, regroups, and transforms the meanings in the light of the situation in which he is placed and the direction of his action" (Blumer 1969, 5). In addition, it should be noted that "interpretation should not be regarded as a mere automatic application of established meanings, but as a formative process in which meanings are used and revised as instruments for the guidance and formation of action" (Blumer 1969, 5). With this being said, "it is necessary to see that meanings play their part in action through a process of self-interaction" (Blumer 1969, 5).

Root Images

Though these three basic premises provide an overview of the definition of symbolic interactionism, there is much more to it than that. In *Symbolic Interactionism: Perspective and Method* (1969), Blumer investigated "a number of basic ideas, or "root images" (6) that further depict and describe the ideas that represent the symbolic interactionist perspective. The next section of this investigation into the definition of classical symbolic interactionism will provide an overview of the "root images that refer to and depict the nature of the following matters; human groups or societies, social interaction, objects, the human being as an actor, human action, and the interconnection of the lines of action" (Blumer 1969, 6).

The Nature of Human Group Life

The first basic "root image" of symbolic interactionism is titled the "nature of human group life" (Blumer 1969, 6). According to Blumer, "human groups are seen as consisting of human beings who are engaging in action. Human action consists of the multitudinous activities that individuals perform in their lives as they encounter one another and as they deal with the succession of situations confronting them" (Blumer 1969, 6). Thus, human action is not merely based upon what we do as individuals, as often indicated in psychology. Instead, human action occurs on an individual level, a group level, and a societal level.

Blumer takes this idea one step further when he states that "activities belong to the acting individuals and are carried on by them always with regard to the situations in which they have to act" (Blumer 1969, 6). This means that from a symbolic interactionist perspective, human action and activities are not only derived from several different social levels, but they are also dependent on the situation and context of the situation at hand. Thus, in symbolic interactionism, society can be understood through *action*.

It is contended that deviations occur within culture and social structure. In sociology, the concept of culture is based on what people do. Conversely, the concept of society refers to the interactions and relations between people and how they act toward each other. This combination of culture and society represents the "complex ongoing activity that establishes and portrays structure or organization" (Blumer 1969, 7).

Though the combination of culture and society plays an important role in our actions and activities, it falls short in one aspect of the basic ideas of symbolic interactionism. This is because at the core of symbolic interactionism is based on human interaction. While it can be studied empirically, the human condition, or the qualitative component is paramount to any quantifiable assessment. Blumer advances that to be empirically valid, the assessment must be consistent with the nature of the social action of human beings (Blumer 1969, 7). This is the case whether we are engaged in culture or society, the process in which we derive our actions and activities is based within a constant ongoing process that is contextual (situational).

Nature of Social Interaction

In what is referred to as the "nature of social interaction" (Blumer 1969, 7), it is argued that human social interaction, regardless of culture, takes place within groups that can be either small or large in character. In this sense, our life consists of groups and groups contain individual lives. This point is made when Blumer advances that society consists of individuals interacting with one another" (Blumer 1969, 7). This lack of significance can be seen in the social sciences, especially in the areas of psychology and sociology. It happens in these fields because both social sciences often define social interaction as the effects of outside factors or forces. For example, sociology attributes social interaction as behavior influenced by factors such as social status, norms, values, sanctions, role demands, and stressors. Psychology tends to attribute social interaction to factors such as motives, attitudes and hidden complexes, once again making the individual passive or more likely to be influenced by outside stressors or internal pressures to adapt to outside influences.

The one-way process of social interaction that both psychology and sociology use to explain human behavior does not fit the conceptual ideas of symbolic interactionism. They do not fit because each of these social sciences is suggesting that social interaction is secondary, or the effect of sociological or psychological determinants move to bring about given forms of human behavior" (Blumer 1969, 7). Blumer recognizes social interaction to be of vital importance insofar as it is a process that determines human conduct, rather than passively serving as an effect of outside influences (Blumer 1969, 8). Individuals have to take into account what others are doing and thus engage in conduct or actions to address their situations accordingly

In summary, symbolic interactionism focuses on how "a human society or group consists of people in association. Such association exists necessarily in the form of people acting toward one another and thus engaging in social interaction" (Blumer 1969, 10). The interactions that humans participate in are "characteristically and predominately on the symbolic level; as individuals acting individually, collectively, as agents of some organization encounter one another they are necessarily required to take account of the actions of one another as they form their own action" (Blumer 1969, 10). This is done on a daily basis through "a dual process of indicating to others how to act and of interpreting the indications made by others" (Blumer 1969, 10).

Nature of Objects

Blumer's third "root image" of symbolic interactionism can be found in the "Nature of Objects" (Blumer 1969, 10). In the symbolic interactionist perspective, "the 'worlds' that exist for human beings and for their groups are composed of 'objects'; these objects are the product of symbolic interactionism" (Blumer 1969, 10). According to Blumer, an object can be defined as "anything that can be indicated, anything that is pointed to or referred to—a cloud, a book, a legislature, a banker, a religious doctrine, a ghost, and so forth" (Blumer 1969, 10). The "objects" that Blumer discusses can be arranged into three separate categories: (1) "Physical objects, such as chairs, trees, or bicycles"; (2) "Social objects, such as students, priests, a president, a mother, or a friends, and"; (3) "Abstract objects, such as moral principles, philosophical doctrines, or ideas such as justice, exploration, or compassion" (Blumer 1969, 10–11).

For Blumer, the nature an "object," regardless of which category it may fall into, "consists of the meaning that it has for the person for whom it is an object" (Blumer 1969, 11). That is, "meaning sets the way in which he sees the object, the way in which he is prepared to act toward it, and the way in which he is ready to talk about it" (Blumer 1969, 11). In addition, "an object may have a different meaning for different individuals" (Blumer 1969, 11). An example of this can be seen in everyday life: an animal means something different to a zoologist, a person passing by this animal, the people at animal control, and an artist's rendition of the animal at hand. In each of these cases, the animal that stands before them means something quite different to each person.

This is not to say that "objects" are derived merely from individual interpretation or opinions of the "object" at hand. In fact, "the meanings of objects for a person can arise fundamentally out of the way they are defined to him by others with whom he interacts" (Blumer 1969, 11). Blumer takes this statement one step further and proclaims that "out of a process of mutual indications common objects emerge—objects that have the same meaning for a given set of people and are seen in the same manner by them" (Blumer 1969, 11).

This perspective, the symbolic interactionist perspective, of "objects," has several larger implications that are not immediately apparent from this discussion. One implication of Blumer's view on "objects" is that it challenges the traditional notion that "the environment consists *only* of objects that the given human being recognizes and knows" (Blumer 1969, 11). In symbolic interactionism, "the nature of this environment (world) is set by the meaning that the objects composing it have for those human beings" (Blumer 1969, 11). This means that "in order to understand the action of people it is necessary to identify their world of objects" (Blumer 1969, 110)

The second implication of this perspective on "objects" is that "objects" (in the sense of their meaning) must be seen as social creation—as being formed in and arising out of the process of definition and interpretation as this process takes place in the interaction of people" (Blumer 1969, 11–12). The point Blumer makes with this statement that "the meaning of anything and everything has to be formed, learned, and transmitted through a process of indication—a process that is necessarily a social process" (Blumer 1969, 12). Overall, this means that the perspective of symbolic interactionism views "human group life as a process in which objects are being created, affirmed, transformed, and cast aside. This, in turn, also means that the life and action of people change in line with the changes taking place in their world of objects" (Blumer 1969, 12).

Humans as Acting Organisms

The fourth "root image" of symbolic interactionism falls under the section titled, "The Human Being as an Acting Organism" (Blumer 1969, 12). As stated earlier, "SI recognizes that human beings must have a makeup that fits the nature of social interaction" (Blumer 1969, 12). Also, as stated earlier, a "human being is seen as an organism that not only responds to others on the non-symbolic level but as one that makes indications to others and interprets their indications" (Blumer 1969, 12). These two statements, detached from one another, do not mean much. However, if you synthesize both of these symbolic interactionist statements, the formation of a "self" or the idea that "human beings can be the object of their own actions" (Blumer 1969, 12) begins to emerge.

Not only do human beings possess the ability to be objects of their own actions, but they can also "recognize themselves, for instance, a person can see himself as being a man, young in age, a student, in debt, trying to become a doctor, coming from an undistinguished family and so forth" (Blumer 1969, 12). In each of the aforementioned examples, a person can be "an object to oneself and act towards one self and guide oneself in their actions towards others on the basis of the kind of object you are to yourself" (Blumer 1969, 12). Though the "self" is a different type of object, it still retains a very important property that the other categorized objects possess, and that is that "like other objects the self-object emerges from the process of social interaction in which other people are defining a person to himself" (Blumer 1969, 12).

The "self" that human beings develop not only functions as an object, but it also "enables humans to interact with themselves" (Blumer 1969, 13). This interaction with one's own self—a sort of internal conversation—has nothing to do with psychologically being between two minds or being between two distinct sets of concepts, ideas, notions, attitudes, feelings, etc. "Instead, the interaction is social—a form of communication with the person addressing himself as a person and responding thereto" (Blumer 1969, 13). According to Blumer, "we can clearly recognize such interaction in ourselves as each of us notes that he is angry with himself, or that he has to spur himself on in his tasks, or that he reminds himself to do this or that, or that he is talking to himself in working out some plan of action" (Blumer 1969, 13). Whenever humans participate in these self-interactions, they are essentially "making indications to oneself" (Blumer 1969, 13). These indications take place in our everyday lives on a grand scale; Blumer makes this point when he states that "one's waking life consists of a series of such indications that the person is making to himself" (Blumer 1969, 13).

Uniqueness of the Nature of Human Action

The fifth "root image" of symbolic interactionism centers on the very "Nature of Human Action" itself (Blumer 1969, 15). According to Blumer, the nature of human action is unique because "the capacity of human beings to make indications to themselves gives a distinctive character to human action" (Blumer 1969, 15). This distinctive character "means that the human individual confronts a world that he must interpret in order to act instead of an environment to which he responds because of his organization" (Blumer 1969, 15).

The position that symbolic interactionism takes on human action focuses on how "people have to cope with the situations in which they are called on to act, ascertaining the meaning of the actions of others mapping out our own line of action in the light of such interpretation" (Blumer 1969, 15). This, in turn, means that "people have to construct and guide their actions instead of merely releasing [them] in response to factors playing on them or operating through them; even though humans may do a miserable job in constructing their actions, they are indeed able to construct them" (Blumer 1969, 15). The symbolic interactionist perspective on human action "stands sharply in contrast to the view of human action that dominates current psychological and social sciences" (Blumer 1969, 15).

Though the symbolic interactionist perspective on action differs vastly from the traditional views of social science, it is still *incomplete*. One aspect of the nature of human action that must be taken into account is that the process involves situations in which they are compelled to engage in, but how they assess it and how they proceed with action is based on what they individually configure. A second aspect of the nature of human action that must be taken into account is that one must get inside of the defining processes of the individual in order to understand her/his action. That process of defining meaning, and engaging in specific action is governed by internal mechanisms that deal with outside influences or stressors and it cannot always be predicted.

These views are argued to apply to the individual social actor as well as groups. Blumer advances that groups also collectively are engaged in an interpretative process where the collectivity is called on to act. Collectives can include armies that engage in battles, corporations seeking to expand their operations, or a nation-state trying to address an unfavorable imbalance in trade. In these examples, the collective needs to construct its action through an interpretation of what is occurring in its area of operation. Specifically, the interpretative process involves social actors making indications to one another. Joint or collective action is an outcome of interpretive interaction.

Interlinkage of Action

The sixth and final "root image" is the "Interlinkage of Action" (Blumer 1969, 16). As stated earlier, "human group life consists of, and exists in, the fitting of lines of action to each other by the members of the group" (Blumer 1969, 16– 17). These "lines of action give rise to and constitute "joint action"—a societal organization of conduct of different acts of diverse participants" (Blumer 1969, 17). The "joint actions" that Blumer discusses can be described as having "a distinctive character in their own right, a character that lies in the articulation or linkage as apart from what may be articulated or linked" (Blumer 1969, 17). This means that "joint action" can be assessed and discussed without breaking each action into separate parts or pieces.

Examples of this principle are illustrated in everyday life "when we speak of such things as marriage, a trading transaction, war, a parliamentary discussion, or a church service" (Blumer 1969, 17). Examples such as these allow symbolic interactionists "to speak of the collectivity—that humans engage in joint action without having to identify the individual members of that collectivity" (Blumer 1969, 17). This symbolic interactionist conception of "joint action" should be the focus and "domain of the social scientist" (Blumer 1969, 17).

As important as the study of "joint action" should be to social science, Blumer warns that there are problems which every researcher must avoid. The first warning that he issues is that "in dealing with collectivities and with joint action one can easily be trapped in an erroneous position by failing to recognize that the joint action of the collectivity is an inter-linkage of the separate acts of the participants" (Blumer 1969, 17). This oversight made by many social scientists and researchers "leads [them] to overlook the fact that a joint action always has to undergo a process of formation; even though it may be a well-established and repetitive form of social action, each instance of it has to be formed anew" (Blumer 1969, 17).

The second warning that Blumer issues about "joint-action" is that "this career of formation through which it (action) comes into being necessarily takes place through the dual process of designation and interpretation" (Blumer 1969, 17). This being said, "the participants (whether collectively or individually) have to guide their respective acts by forming and using meanings" (Blumer 1969, 17). With the admittance of these two common mistakes made when studying "joint action," we can now move on two a more advanced study of the subject.

In the final section of Blumer's investigation into the sixth "root image," the "Interlinkage of Action" (Blumer 1969, 16), he makes three observations into what constitutes joint action (Blumer 1969, 17). The first observation he makes centers on the idea that joint action can be both repetitive and stable (Blumer 1969, 17). Blumer advances that social action is based on recurrent patterns of joint action" (Blumer 1969, 17). Specifically, Blumer suggests that individuals have a pre-conceived mapping of most situations in that they understand how to act and how others will act. Overall, this means that the majority of our joint actions toward our self and others is pre-planned. This happens because individuals are compelled to interact with other individuals, or groups who share common and established meanings of what is expected in the action of participants. Individuals are thus guided to conform to and guide their own behavior by such meanings of what is constituted as acceptable behavior of the majority.

His second observation on the subject of interlinkage in relation to "joint action" deals with the notion that an "extended connection of actions makes up much of human group life" Blumer 1969, 19). According to Blumer, "we are familiar with these large complex networks of action involving an interlinkage and interdependency of diverse actions of diverse people—as in the division of labor" (Blumer 1969, 19). For example, there is an extended group of actions involved in a dairy farmer milking a cow and the milk's eventual arrival at a store. However, examples and instances of extended group actions preoccupy a greater importance in social science than applying to the here and now, the everyday. These actions "also give substance to the idea that human group life has the character of a system" (Blumer 1969, 19).

The third and final point about "joint action" is "that any instance of joint action, whether newly formed or long established has necessarily risen out of a background of previous actions of the participants" (Blumer 1969, 20). In essence, this means that "a new kind of joint action never comes into existence apart from such a background" (Blumer 1969, 20). This, in turn, means that "the participants involved in the formation of a new joint action always bring to that formation the world of objects, the sets of meanings, and the schemes of interpretation that they already possess" (Blumer 1969, 20). In sum, "joint action always emerges out of and is connected with a context of previous action" (Blumer 1969, 20).

Conclusions

The definition of symbolic interactionism that Blumer presents in *Symbolic Interactionism: Perspective and Method* (1969) represents an attempt at systematically laying out the major core concepts of the perspective known as symbolic interactionism. Not only does Blumer focus on defining the term, he elaborates the "root images" that sharpen and clarify the backbone of the perspective. While many other definitions for symbolic interactionism exist, there are two major reasons why Blumer's ideas are central to the research at hand.

The first reason Blumer's definition, core concepts, and root images are of primary interest to this research is because none of the other earlier scholars presented a systematic approach. Blumer's *Symbolic Interactionism: Perspective and Method* (1969) represents "the basic premises of the point of view and to develop['s] the methodological consequences for the studying of human group life" (Blumer 1969, 78). In sum, Blumer's overall aim/goal of laying out the principles and roots of symbolic interactionism was accomplished through this work. The second major reason for using the definition "root images" as discussed by Blumer and examining Royce's contributions to its early development core ideas of symbolic interactionism has to do with the time period in which Blumer wrote.

It should be noted at this point in the discussion of Blumer that since the intent of this research is to investigate symbolic interactionist theory a discussion of all the varieties within the SI perspective, though somewhat important, seems inappropriate. There are four major schools or varieties of symbolic interactionism: "the Chicago school (Blumer, Park, Mead, etc.), the Iowa school (Kuhn), the Dramaturgical approach (Goffman), and ethnomethodology (Garfinkel)" (Meltzer, Petras and Reynolds 1980, 54). But these four unique veins symbolic interactionist thought reflect more modern versions of the symbolic interactionist perspective. That is, these four types/varieties of symbolic interactionism were created and developed well after Royce's time and Blumer's systematic defining of the symbolic interactionist perspective. Thus, definitions and systematic explanations of symbolic interactionism based upon these four varieties of symbolic interactionist hold little weight in this analysis of the works of Royce in relation to the development symbolic interactionist thought.

The two major reasons for using Blumer's conception of symbolic interactionism are that Blumer's definition postdates the early symbolic interactionists (James, Dewey, Mead, etc.) by a few decades and predates the varieties or numerous veins of interactionist thought. This means that Blumer's conceptual ideas on the perspective of symbolic interactionism lie between two developmentally important time periods.

The unique situation of Blumer's ideas falling between both time frames provides an explanation and understanding of symbolic interactionism that can assist in relating Royce's later academic works to classical symbolic interactionism while avoiding the problem of incorporating veins of symbolic interactionist thought that, by far, postdate Royce's and Blumer's work. In addition, it circumvents a second problem: the problem of defining symbolic interactionism in relation to a post-modern explanation of the perspective.

Overall, the definition and explanation of symbolic interactionism that Blumer presents provides the backbone of what is meant by the term symbolic interactionism. Blumer's highly organized and systematic treatment of the subject allows for Royce's later academic work in relation to symbolic interactionism to be compared and contrasted with relative ease. By focusing on Royce's academic works, *The Problem of Christianity* (1913) and "Mind" (1916) and relating them to the outline of Blumer's definition and "root images" of symbolic interactionism, the contribution that Royce made to symbolic interactionist thought becomes clear.

CHAPTER IX

COMPARING THE IDEAS
OF ROYCE AND BLUMER

This chapter is split into two distinct sections. The first section compares and contrasts the later writings of Royce and Blumer's definition of symbolic interactionism and its "root images." The second section of this chapter presents a discussion of the similarities and differences between Blumer's and Royce's theoretical ideas. Based on these research findings, a judgment about Royce's contribution will be assessed and deliberated. The final results and assessment lead us to a definitive answer to the question of whether Royce made a contribution to early symbolic interactionism.

Royce and the Premises of Symbolic Interactionism

As stated earlier in Blumer's definition of symbolic interactionism, there are three major premises:

[1.] "Human beings act toward things on the basis of the meanings that the things have for them" (Blumer 1969, 2).

[2.] "The meaning of such things is derived from, or arises out of, the social interaction that one has with one's fellows" (Blumer 1969, 2).

[3.] "These meanings are handled in, and modified through, an interpretive process used by the person in dealing with the things he encounters" (Blumer 1969, 2).

First Premise

Royce illustrates the first premise that people act based upon meaning, in *The Problem of Christianity* (1913). For Royce, a practical example of the first premise can be found in his situation at a signpost. "When you observe, at a crossing of roads, a sign-post, you will never discover what the real sign-post is, either by continuing to perceive it, or by merely conceiving its structure or its relations to any perceived objects, or to any merely abstract laws in heaven or in earth" (Royce 1968, 346). This means that you cannot "learn what the sign-post is by any process of watching in the course of your individual experience the "workings" of any ideas that it suggests to you" (Royce 1968, 347). The only way in which you can "understand" the sign-post is "if you learn to read it" (Royce 1968, 347). Not only must you learn to read, but you must also consider that the "very being of a sign-post consists in its nature as a guide, needing interpretation, and pointing the way" (Royce 1968, 347).

The signpost, for Royce, is "constituted of at least three distinct minds" (Royce 1968, 347): "The mind whose intention to point out the way is expressed in the construction of the sign-post...the mind to which the sign-post actually points out the way"; however, the sign's meaning is not made clear to this mind unless he or she knows how to read, and the "third mind which interprets the sign—post to the inquiring wayfarer (traveler). The wayfarer (traveler), if he knows how to read, may be his own interpreter" (Royce 1968, 347).

Royce takes his example of the signpost one step further when he considers the "three distinct mental functions" (1968, 347) or "three minds" involved in interpreting the signpost. First, there's "the function of the mind whose purpose the sign expresses" (Royce 1968, 347). Second, "there is the mind which is guided by the interpretation of the sign" (Royce 1968, 347). Lastly, there "is the function of the interpreter to whom the reading of the sign is due" (Royce 1968, 347).

The example of the signpost and the complex process of interpreting the meaning of the sign represent the point that Blumer is trying to make in his first premise – "that human beings act toward things on the basis of the meanings that the things have for them" (Royce 1969, 2). By interpreting the meaning of the sign, based upon the "three minds" and "three mental functions," a person is able to derive the meaning of not only the context of the situation, but also, and most importantly, the sign itself. Thus, for Royce, humans act upon the interpretation of a sign and its meaning(s). In the case of the signpost, a person would interpret the sign and its meaning (externally) and then act accordingly.

A second example of people acting upon the meaning of the world around them comes from an internal example. In *The Problem of Christianity* (1913), Royce discussed the meaning of facial expressions in relation to one's neighbor. "For, as a fact, I know very little about my own facial expressions, except what I learn, if indeed I learn at all, through accepting as true certain reports of my neighbors regarding these facial expressions" (Royce 1968, 359). However, this does not mean one cannot look at one's face in the mirror and indirectly perceive one's facial expressions although this cannot yield any knowledge about "what [my] own changes of facial expression are" (Royce 1968, 359). Since people cannot rely on the facial expressions observed in the mirror people have to interpret the signs of others. According to Royce, we have "spent years of our lives interpreting the signs which we have read as we looked at the countenances of other men" (Royce 1968, 359).

This example, though basic, is "typical for the way in which we interpret the usual signs of his mind which our neighbor gives to us" (Royce 1968, 359). This is in large part true because "I never normally view my own organism in a perspective which is closely analogous to the perspective in which I constantly perceive the body and the movements of my fellow man" (Royce 1968, 359). Overall, since we cannot know our selves through our own interpretations alone, "our most important knowledge about our own expressive movements comes to us at second hand. We learn how our own movements appear through the report of others" (Royce 1968, 359).

This example of interpreting our facial expressions leads to a secondary facet of meaning—the idea that people derive meaning from interpretations on both an external and internal level. The interpretive process Royce discussed in relation to facial expressions illustrates two major points: First, that the human ability to interpret can assist in understanding the meaning or meanings of our neighbors, and second, the understanding and deriving of meaning from the interpretation of neighbors can assist in creating "self" meaning and understanding. This synthesis of internal and external meaning, along with the process of interpretation involved in understanding ourselves and others, creates a philosophy that makes meaning important in its own right. This is a point that Blumer makes when he states that "the position of symbolic interactionism is that the meaning that things have for human beings are central in their own right" (Blumer 1969, 3). This shared idea between Blumer's first premise and Royce's philosophy is the beginning of Royce's connection to early symbolic interactionism.

Deriving Meaning from Social Interactions

Blumer's second major premise is "that the meaning of such things is derived from, or arises out of, the social interaction that one has with one's fellows" (Blumer 1969, 2). For Blumer, meaning is created from a social process or a process of social interaction that takes place between humans. This is a statement he clarifies when he says that the symbolic interactionist perspective "sees meaning as arising out of the process of interaction between people" (Blumer 1969, 4). Basically, this means symbolic interactionists view "the meaning of a thing for a person as growing out of the ways in which other persons act toward the person with regard to the thing; this also means that actions operate to define the thing for the person" (Blumer 1969, 4), a point that Royce also makes.

For Royce, creating meaning or understanding from the interpretive process around us is an extremely social undertaking. He states that "Interpretation is the knowledge of the meaning of a sign. Such a knowledge is not a mere apprehension, nor yet a conceptual process; it is the essentially social process whereby the knower at once distinguishes himself, with his own meanings, ideas, and expressions, from some other self, and at the same time knows that these selves have their contrasted meanings, while one of them at the moment is expressing its meaning to the other" (Royce 2001, 63).

This idea of deriving meaning and understanding from others is also clarified when Royce asserts "that interpretation is a conversation and not a lonely enterprise"— meaning that people are constantly engaged in the process of interpreting and assessing meaning and understanding from one another (Royce 1968, 289). In addition, the created meaning stemming from the interpretive process can help in the understanding of the meanings of others' ideas and themselves, as well as one's knowledge of self. Royce announces this point when he proclaims that "the most important part of my knowledge about myself is based upon knowledge that I have derived from the community (society) to which I belong. In particular, my knowledge about the socially expressive moments of my own organism is largely derived from what I learn through the testimony of my *fellow men*" (Royce 1968, 358).

Royce, like Blumer, operates off the very strong notion that the way we interpret the world around us and derive meaning is essentially a process that involves "social interaction with one's fellows" (Blumer 1969, 2). Human interaction with other individuals leads us to a two-way process: people can interpret and derive meaning from others about others, and people can interpret and derive meaning and understanding about themselves from others.

Interpretive Process

The third major premise of symbolic interactionism outlined by Blumer is the idea "that meanings are handled in, and modified through, an interpretive process used by the person in dealing with the things he encounters".(2) This "interpretive process" has two essential parts. "The actor indicates to himself the things toward which he is acting, and he has to point out to himself the things that have meaning" (Blumer 1969, 5). In addition, the creation of such indicators rests in "an internalized social process in that the actor is interacting with himself. This interaction with himself is something other than the interplay of psychological elements; it is an instance of the person engaging in a process of communication with himself" (Blumer 1969, 5).

Royce emphasizes the importance of Blumer's third premise when he states that "if there is no interpreter, there is no interpretation. And if there is no interpretation, there is no world" (Royce 1968, 362). In Royce's later academic writings, he pays particular attention to this idea of a "process of interpretation." For Royce, the process of interpretation is an ongoing process, that is "when once initiated, interpretation can be terminated only by an external and arbitrary interruption, such as death or social separation" (Royce 1968, 290). Thus, for a world to exist, there must be a process of ongoing interpretation that people participate in every day.

Royce further illustrates Blumer's concept of the "interpretive process" and its significance:

> When a man understands a spoken or written word or sentence, what he perceives is some sign, or expression of an idea or meaning, which in general belong to the mind of some fellow man. When this sign or expression is understood by the one who hears or who reads, what is made present to the consciousness of the reader or hearer may be any combination of perceptual or conceptual knowledge that chances to be in question...However, my 'grasping of his idea', consists neither in the percept of the sign nor in the concept of its object which the sign arouses, but in my interpretation of the sign as an indication of an idea which is distinct from any idea of mine (Royce 2001, 60).

This quotation describes one-half of Blumer's third major premise. Royce puts an emphasis on dealing with the interpretation and understanding of the meaning of other's ideas. However, Royce also made an effort to point out that objects can be signs that need interpretation. We see a clear example of this within the signpost example. The signpost in Royce's example presents itself to a wayward traveler. The sign that lies before the traveler needs interpretation to indicate its meaning. According to Royce, the "very being of a sign-post consists in its nature as a guide, needing interpretation, and pointing the way" (Royce 1968, 347). Royce takes his example a step further when he suggests that "our experience, as it comes to us, is a realm of signs. That is, the facts of our experience resemble sign-posts" (Royce 1968, 347). This means that in relation to our everyday lives, the world consists of little signposts everywhere; these signposts, like all other signs, need to be interpreted. Royce clarifies this point when he says that "the real world contains the interpreter of these signs, and the very being of the world consists in the truth of the interpretation, in the whole realm of experience, these signs obtain" (Royce 1968, 348).

Thus far, half of Blumer's third major premise, in relation to Royce's later academic works, has been discussed. There is a component of Royce's philosophy that focuses on interpreting the meaning of other's ideas and objects around us; however, the second half of Blumer's third premise, the idea that we also interpret meaning from within or internally, has yet to be discussed This switch from a process of interpretation to a more internalized process is a transition that Royce made.

The best explanation of Royce's philosophy on internal interpretation comes from his answer to his question "Why do I postulate others' minds?" (Royce 1968, 360). In *The Problem of Christianity* (1913), he answers this question by stating, "I postulate your mind, first, because, when you address me, by word or gesture, you arouse in me ideas which, by virtue of their contrast with my ideas, and by virtue of their own novelty and their unexpectedness, I know to be not any ideas of my own" (Royce 1968, 360). This is an important point for Royce because when people encounter ideas other than their own, they "first try, however they can, to interpret those ideas which are not theirs" (Royce 1968, 360). These encountered ideas, that are interpreted, represent a cognitive or mental process of interpretation.

This mental process of interpretation takes place when "new ideas...words, and deeds are suggested to me that actually require an interpretation" (Royce 1968, 360). These ideas that constantly come into the human mind require two specific things: "an interpreter" and "an interpretation" (Royce 1968, 360). The interpreter plays a major role in "mediating between the new ideas which your deeds have suggested to me, and the trains of ideas which I already call my own" (Royce 1968, 360). After having mediated between both sets of ideas, the interpreter "would compare all these ideas, and would both observe and express wherein lay their contrast and its meaning. Now such an interpreter, mediating between two contrasting ideas or sets of ideas, and making clear their contrasts, their meaning, and their mutual relations, would be, by hypothesis, a mind" (Royce 1968, 360).

The mind that Royce describes is a mind that exists internally and functions to interpret the world around us. This point is illustrated when he states that "interpretation is a mental act" or moreover, that interpretation requires the use of an internal mental interpretive process (Royce 1968, 289). Royce provides an example of this point when he makes the statement that "whenever in memory we review our own past, when we reflect upon our own meaning, when we form a plan, or when we ask ourselves what we mean or engage in any inner conversation which forms the commonest of expressions of the activity whereby an individual man attains some sort of explicit knowledge of himself" (Royce 2001, 62).

In relation to the second half of Blumer's third premise of the definition of symbolic interactionism, Royce's writings contain an interpretive process that includes communication with oneself about interpreting the various elements of the world. These elements, as outlined above, can range from interpreting a neighbor's ideas or interpreting objects or signposts, to interpreting an individual's own ideas internally. In sum, when all the aspects of Royce's conceptions of the process of interpretation are put together, there is definitely a connection between his writings and those stated in Blumer's third premise.

Royce and the Root Images

The second half of this chapter relates the later academic works of Royce: *The Problem of Christianity* (1913), and "Mind" (1916) to the "root images" that Blumer described in *Symbolic Interactionism: Perspective and Method* (1969). Though these "root images" are not as involved as the three major premises, their use in this research provides a more in-depth look into the philosophy of Royce in relation to the development of early symbolic interactionist thought. Hence, this comparison provides additional vital information that will assist in the final assessment of the question: did Royce make a significant contribution to the development of symbolic interactionism?

The first "root image" that Blumer discusses is the idea that "human groups are seen as consisting of human beings who are engaging in action" (Blumer 1969, 6). Blumer takes this idea one step further stating that "human action consists of the multitudinous activities that individuals perform in their lives as they encounter one another and as they deal with the succession of situations confronting them" (Blumer 1969, 6). Basically, Blumer suggests that the world around us consists of action or actions that must be assessed by the situations within which they are encountered.

An example of this concept is illustrated by Royce who discussed the real-life situation of reading and interpreting of a signpost. In the example, a sign-post presents itself to a wayward traveler. The traveler, who is able to read, must interpret the sign within the context it exists. Next, the traveler must make a decision as to what the signpost means through the process of interpretation. Finally, the traveler must choose which direction to follow and then follow it to the end or until another signpost appears.

In this particular example, Royce is illustrating the point that interpreting the world around us and making decisions based upon our understanding of meaning is a persistent feature of our daily lives. He emphasizes this when he states that "the facts of our experience resemble sign-posts," (that is, our world consists of interpreting the signposts of our daily lives (Royce 1968, 347). These signposts that need and require the process of interpretation lie at the "very being of the universe and it consists in a process whereby the world is interpreted, in indeed in its wholeness, at any one moment of time but through an infinite series of acts of interpretation" (Royce 1968, 346). The sign-posts that present themselves in everyday life both describe and represent the various situations and activities that lie before us. In addition, the signposts and situations that present themselves in everyday life require interpretation. This "process of interpretation," as it has come to be referred to, is also a persistent and infinite feature of human life. This illustration only addresses one half of Blumer's first "root image" and even though Royce does not specifically mention human groups this does not mean that groups do not preoccupy a place in his philosophy is discussed below.

Social Interaction

The second "root image" Blumer presents is the concept that "group life necessarily presupposes interaction between the group members; or, put otherwise, a society consists of individuals interacting with one another" (Blumer 1969, 7). The clearest example of this concept that Royce offers can be found in his discussion on the "community of interpretation." For Royce, interpretation and the process of interpreting signs, signposts, and a, objects, which will be discussed later, plays a major role in life. Royce takes this notion one step further by discussing the interpretive process in terms of deriving meaning from signs, other humans, and ourselves (internal interpretation). The final component of Royce's interpretive process is the notion that people live within a "community of interpretation."

The "community of interpretation" that Royce discusses can be defined as: "If, then I am worthy to be an interpreter at all we three you, my neighbor, whose mind I would fain interpret, you, my kindly listener, to whom I am, address my interpretation, -we three constitute a Community. Let us give this community a technical name, let us call it a 'Community of Interpretation'" (Royce 1968, 315). The point Royce makes within the above quotation centers on his notion of a larger group within which interpretation takes place.

This relates to Blumer's second "root image" because, according to Royce, the process of interpretation "is not only an essentially social process, but also a process which, when once initiated, can be terminated only by an external and arbitrary interruption, such as death or social separation" (Royce 1968, 290). Therefore, interpretation is a social process that has roots in both the individual world (the signpost example) and the larger group world. However, there is a line that must be drawn between Royce's and Blumer's conception of the second "root image."

The difference between Royce's and Blumer's take on the topic of individual and group interaction lies in the concept of interpretation. In the case of Blumer, when he talks about group and individual interaction, it is meant as a blanket statement. For instance, I interact with a neighbor, and last week my neighbors threw a party and I talked to several people in my courtyard. This is the type of group and individual interaction that Blumer refers to in his second "root image."

Royce differs from Blumer in that he discusses individual and group interactions in relation to their function and uses within a process of interpretation. This process of interpretation is expanded upon in the "doctrine of signs" literature when Royce discusses a "community of interpretation." For Royce, "in this world of interpretation, of whose most general structure we have now obtained a glimpse, selves and communities may exist" (Royce 1968, 294). This quotation illustrates Royce's idea that the process of interpretation involves both individuals and communities that can consist of a small group (a handful of people) or a larger community (potentially society). Overall, this means that Royce realized that there are individual and group interactions.

Objects

The third "root image" Blumer presented is the notion that "the "worlds" that exist for human beings and for their groups are composed of "objects"; these objects are the product of symbolic interactionism" (Blumer 1969, 10). Blumer expands this idea stating that an object can be defined as "anything that can be indicated, anything that is pointed to or referred to—a cloud, a book, a legislature, a banker, a religious doctrine, a ghost, and so forth" (Blumer 1969, 10). This concept of "objects" is split into three categories by Blumer: observable (physical) objects, social objects, and abstract objects.

In the works of Royce, there appears to be a similar notion of Blumer's "objects" contained within the term "signs." At first, Royce decided to use the conceptualization of sign created by Peirce that he describes as being "the name for an object to which somebody gives or should give an interpretation" (Royce 1968, 344). Though very direct, Royce did not see Peirce's conceptualization as workable because it does not cover all the bases. For Royce, a sign can be "something that determines an interpretation" and can "also be called an expression of a mind; and, in our social intercourse, it actually is such an expression" (Royce 1968, 345). Royce takes his conceptualization one step further stating that "one might say that a sign is, in its essence, either a mind or a quasi-mind, an object that fulfills the function of a mind" (Royce 1968, 345). Thus far, the objects/signs that Royce discussed have been social and abstract types of objects.

Royce does not leave out physical objects because he believes that signs should be applicable to everyday life and everyday situations. He makes this point when he states that "a word, a clock-face, a weather-vane, or a gesture is a sign" (Royce 1968, 345). The inclusion of this statement in Royce's writings causes him to conceptualize a sign as "an object whose being consists in the fact that the sign calls for an interpretation" (Royce 1968, 345). This definition will lead back to a familiar compromise between the concept of an object (Blumer) and the concept of a sign (Royce).

The objects that Blumer refers to are stand-alone objects in their own right—nothing more, nothing less. For Royce, the objects or signs that present themselves in everyday life play an essential role in the interpretive process. Once again, the difference between the concepts of "objects" and "signs" appears to be their overall function in daily life. For Blumer, the objects are just there, while for Royce, the signs that present themselves are part of a larger process—the interpretive process that preoccupies our entire life. This does not mean that there is not a link between Blumer's "objects" and Royce's "signs," as both refer to objects/signs as being part of the symbolic process.

Interpreting Indications

The fourth "root image" focuses on the notion that "a human being is seen as an organism that not only responds to others on the non-symbolic level, but as one that makes indications to others and interprets their indications" (Blumer 1969, 12). The basis of this "root image" can be seen in Royce's example involving the interpretation of a neighbor's facial expressions.

In *The Problem of Christianity* (1913), Royce makes the following statement: "The appearance of my fellow's countenance is to me a sign of his mind. And signs of this type stand in the front rank of those facts of perception upon which my customary interpretation of his mind depends whenever he and I are in each other's presence" (Royce 1968, 358). Royce's quotation aims at the heart of Blumer's fourth "root image" and the idea that people interpret one another's indications. This point is further clarified when Royce discusses his example of interpreting his own facial expressions in relation to his neighbor's reactions.

According to Royce, "as a fact, I know very little about my own facial expressions, except what I learn, if indeed I learn at all, through accepting as true certain reports of my neighbors regarding these facial expressions" (Royce 1968, 359). Though a person could merely observe [their] facial expressions in a mirror, this will not yield any knowledge about "what [their] own changes of facial expression are" (Royce 1968, 359). Since people cannot rely on the observed facial expressions from a mirror alone, they are left with interpreting the signs of others. Royce makes this point when he states that we have "spent years of our lives interpreting the signs which we have read as we looked at the countenances of other men" (Royce 1968, 359). In conclusion, this leads Royce to believe that "our most important knowledge about our own expressive movements comes to us at second hand. We learn how our own movements appear through the report of others" (Royce 1968, 359).

In sum, Royce puts an enormous focus on the idea of interpreting the indications of others. Responding to a neighbor's reactions based upon facial expressions is an example that people deal with on an everyday basis. Royce's example was meant to be basic and because it illustrates his point at a level that is not only easily applicable to our daily lives but also shows the persistence of such a feature in daily life. In relation to Blumer's fourth "root image," Royce's concept of interpreting indications serves the same function as Blumer's concept. They are the same because both reflect a process of interpretation and both see the fourth "root image" as a normal aspect of human life.

Human Action

Blumer's fifth "root image" takes the position that "people have to cope with the situations in which they are called on to act, ascertaining the meaning of the actions of others mapping out our own line of action in the light of such interpretation" (Blumer 1969, 15). Blumer's concept of acting, creating meaning, and interpreting the world around us can be seen in Royce's academic works in relation to three major areas.

The first major example of Blumer's fifth "root image" can be found in Royce's metaphor of the world as a collection of signposts. For Royce, the world around us consists of little signposts that he mentions in relation to a signpost in front of a wayward traveler. The traveler must stop and interpret the meaning of the signpost in order to derive what action should be taken next. Examples like the sign-post play a large part in our daily lives; in fact, they play such a large part that Royce claims that "the facts of experience resemble sign-posts. You can never exhaustively find out what they are by resorting either to perception or to conception" (Royce 1968, 347) a process of interpretation must be involved.

The second major example can be found in Royce's example of interpreting individuals own facial expressions. In Royce's example, he discusses how individuals cannot accurately receive a true representation of individual's own facial expressions from just looking into a mirror and perceiving one's facial actions. Instead, people must rely on "interpreting the signs which we have read as we looked at the countenances of other men" (Royce 1968, 359). This process of interpretation involved in facial expressions is very important in that it allows people to interpret the meaning of their facial expressions to others and gives them insight into how to react next.

The third major example comes from Royce's philosophy on the meaning of signs. As stated earlier, Royce defines the concept of a sign as an "object whose being consists in the fact that the sign calls for an interpretation" (Royce 1968, 345). These objects that require interpretation can range from everyday physical objects, to people (social objects), or to ideas or concepts (abstract objects). In addition to a sign being an object that needs interpretation, it also "expresses a mind, and it calls for an interpretation through some other mind, which shall act as mediator between the sign, or between the maker of the sign, and someone to whom the sign is to be read" (Royce 1968, 345). Royce elaborates on this point when he states that "interpreting a sign is, in its turn, the expression of the interpreter's mind, it constitutes a new sign, which again calls for interpretation; and so on without end; unless the process is arbitrarily interrupted" (Royce 1968, 345).

This means that when a person approaches an object or sign, the process of interpretation involved requires an interpreter for the initial sign or object. Next, the interpretive process calls for the interpretation of the meaning or understanding of the object or sign. Lastly, according to Royce, this interpretive process repeats itself until interrupted. Though interruption does happen in our daily lives, it does not mean that the interpretive process is done. This is true for Royce, because "the universe consists of real signs and of their interpretations" (Royce 1968, 345).

In relation to Blumer's fifth "root image," the three sections presented above represent his work on the subject of action through interpretation and meaning. For Royce, there is no separation of the three concepts presented by Blumer, because they occur simultaneously. That is, in the case of the world as signposts, interpreting ourselves and others through facial expressions and the interpretation of signs/objects, there is a shared process of action based upon interpretation and the understanding of their respective meaning.

Joint Action

The final "root image" presented by Blumer deals with the notion that "lines of action give rise to and constitute "joint action" a societal organization of conduct of different acts of diverse participants" (Blumer 1969, 17). These "joint actions," according to Blumer, have "a distinctive character in their own right, a character that lies in the articulation or linkage as apart from what may be articulated or linked" (Blumer 1969, 17). This means that "joint action" cannot be separated into smaller pieces of action.

The only example that Royce provides for this particular concept is the idea of a "community of interpretation." For Royce, the "community of interpretation" involves a process of interpretation that focuses on bringing a group of people's ideas together. An example of this is illustrated when Royce writes, "what I here and now specifically aim to do is this: I mean to interpret you to somebody else, to some other neighbor, who is neither yourself nor myself. Three of us, then, I seek to bring into the desired unity of interpretation" (Royce 1968, 314).

Through this quotation, Royce is attempting an interpretive process where he is taking his interpretation of someone else and presenting it to another person in the hopes of them understanding his words. This is the closest that Royce gets to a description of a joint action. For Royce, there is room to include all three people: himself, the person he is describing, and another neighbor who listens to the description within the conversation.

Keep in mind that Royce allows for the interpretation of signs/objects, which means that his discussion between the people in the conversation could be in reference to the three types of objects: the physical, the social, and the abstract, as previously mentioned.

Though Royce does offer a concept similar to Blumer's concept of "joint action," it does not correspond exactly to the concept that appears in Blumer's conceptualization of symbolic interactionism. In Blumer's version of "joint action," there is a focus on action based upon large scale social institutions, such as religious, political, economic, and family institutions. This does not mean that Royce's discussion on the topic is any less worthy however, in terms of Blumer's sixth "root image," there is no exact comparison.

This marks the end of the section comparing and contrasting Blumer's synthesized conceptualization of symbolic interactionism and Royce's conceptual developments. In the next section, there will be an assessment of Royce's contribution to symbolic interactionism, as well as an examination of what this means for the development of symbolic interactionism and the history of sociology at large. By focusing on these three areas, a clear picture of Royce's contribution to symbolic interactionism emerges. This will provide the evidence that addresses the major question of this book. That is, did Josiah Royce make a contribution to early symbolic interactionism?

CHAPTER X
CONCLUSIONS

Now that Blumer's synthesized conceptualization of symbolic interactionism and Mead's basic ideas on symbolic interactionism have been compared and contrasted to Royce's work we can respond to the question of whether Royce made a significant contribution to the development of early symbolic interactionism. Based upon the evidence presented in this book, Royce did, in fact, make a significant contribution.

Royce's Placement in American Philosophy

Royce grew up, lived, and wrote at the same time as the early pragmatists/symbolic interactionists: Peirce, who lived from 1855 to 1916; James, who lived from 1842 to 1910; and Dewey, who lived from 1859 to 1952. Royce's academic writings did not predate those of the other early pragmatists/ symbolic interactionists. Royce's academic writings did not postdate or exist away from those of the other early pragmatists/symbolic interactionists. Royce's academic pursuits did not develop outside or away from the other early pragmatists/symbolic interactionists.

These four facts place Royce's work within the formative years of early symbolic interactionist thought. By taking a systematic and direct approach to analyzing the connections between Royce and the other early symbolic interactionists, a clear picture emerges and reveals the following main points. The works of Royce cannot be excluded from the events and philosophies that form resulted in the theory of symbolic interactionism. By establishing the historical aspect of Royce's writings and setting the timeframe in which he wrote, an image of Royce as an academic at the epicenter of early symbolic interactionist thought presents itself.

The combination of the two previous points represents an implication about the nature of theory development in relation to symbolic interactionism. That is, the historical timeline of the theory itself, as it stands today, is incomplete. Not only is symbolic interactionist theory incomplete, but it is also lacking. The exclusion of Royce's work, or its conspicuous non-inclusion, throws the notion of a fully understood early symbolic interactionism into contention. The inclusion and recognition of Royce's work in the rich history of symbolic interactionism benefits the theory as a whole. This is the major point to be investigated further in the next section as Royce's later academic works are assessed in relation to the development of symbolic interactionism.

Blumer and Royce: Concluding Thoughts

The first major component in assessing Royce's contribution to symbolic interactionism is based upon his link to the fundamental premises and "root images" of symbolic interactionism as synthesized by Blumer in his book, *Symbolic Interactionism: Perspective and Method* (1969). As previously stated, the choice for using Blumer's conceptualization instead of the numerous alternatives (or varieties of symbolic interactionism) is based on several facts. Blumer's conceptualization falls into a unique category in terms of the development of the early symbolic interactionism time period because it barely postdates the work of the early originators of symbolic interactionism. Yet it predates the establishment of official symbolic interactionism veins or varieties. Blumer's synthesis of the premises and "root images" represents a Herculean effort in attempting to explain the foundations of the theory in a systematic and organized manner. Blumer's synthesis, premises, and "root images" are all inclusive; that is, they include the all-encompassing ideas that create the essential backbone of symbolic interactionism rather than differentiating the theorists or symbolic interactionists who either are or were thought to be the major contributors.

Based upon Blumer's synthesized conceptualization of symbolic interactionism and the later academic works of Royce, the answer to the question of whether Royce made a major contribution to classical symbolic interactionism is an affirmative yes. This affirmation is based on the combined elements of the concepts and ideas that represent symbolic interactionism (Blumer) and the terms, ideas, and concepts that Royce presented in his later academic writings. The synthesis of elements that exist between Blumer and Royce can be highlighted by simply reviewing the connections stated in the earlier chapters.

In terms of Blumer's first premise, that humans act toward meaning, there is a definite connection between Royce and the conceptualizations of the early symbolic interactionists. Royce illustrates this point through his use of examples, such as the signpost that lay ahead for the wayward traveler, and the interpretation of a neighbor's reactions to facial expressions. In both examples, Royce makes the point that individuals are going to base our next act of interpretation on the meaning and understanding of the previous interpretation.

Royce takes this idea one step further when he addresses the issue of "objects" and "signs." This opens up Royce's conception of humans acting based on meaning because it includes physical, social, and abstract modes of deriving meaning. That is, the objects around us are also interpreted, and therefore require understanding and meaning to act upon them. For Royce, humans are constantly basing their next action on the interpreted meaning that lies before them.

Blumer's second major premise, the idea that meaning arises out of a social process, can also be located within the later academic works of Royce. For Royce, the process of interpretation that humans are constantly engaged in "is a conversation and not a lonely enterprise" (Royce 1968, 289). He clarifies this point when he states that "[one's] knowledge about the socially expressive moments of [one's] own organism is largely derived from what I learn through the testimony of my *fellow men*" (Royce 1968, 358). The testimony of fellow men represents the social process of interpreting and deriving meaning.

Blumer's third major premise concerns the importance of a process of interpretation. This is an area of study that Royce elaborated in his later academic writings. The major point Royce makes in *The Problem of Christianity* (1913) and the article "Mind" (1916) centers on the very idea that the process of interpretation is essential. He clarifies this point when he proclaims that "if there is no interpreter, there is no interpretation, and if there is no interpretation, there is no world" (Royce 1968, 362). The emphasis that Blumer places upon the process of interpretation mirrors the importance that Royce attached to the same subject.

The first "root image" Blumer described focuses on how "human groups are seen as consisting of human beings who are engaging in action" (Blumer 1969, 6). In terms of humans engaging in the action of interpretation and deriving meaning, there are instances of this "root image" contained within Royce's concept of a "community of interpretation." The "community of interpretation" involves the interaction of small groups describing and interpreting one another to other people. If a person were in a small group of neighbors, then he or she would be responsible for actively engaging in a conversation of interpretation that could require individual action or group action.

The second "root image" deals with the notion that society is composed of individuals who interact with other societal members. As previously discussed, the interaction that Royce describes between others in the "community of interpretation" differs from Blumer's conception of the idea. The main difference is that, for Royce, small groups and potentially society at large are comprised of individuals and groups in terms of their relation to one another in the interpretive process. Royce did not specifically address this issue in the exact same manner and context that Blumer does.

Blumer's third "root image" focuses on the idea that the world around us consists of objects. For Blumer, objects are split into three categories: physical objects, social objects, and abstract objects. Royce, in a similar fashion, discussed his version of the term "object" in relation to signs. The concept of sign that he created focused on objects that are physical, social, and abstract and are a persistent and constant feature of the world around us.

The fourth "root image" centers on interpreting the actions and indications of other people. An example of interpreting the indications of others can be seen in Royce's facial expression situation. For Royce, interpreting facial expressions in the mirror alone does not yield a lot of information about facial expressions and their perceived meaning. To fully understand and interpret the meaning of facial expressions, people must rely on the indications that other people give them when they are interacting.

The fifth "root image" discussed by Blumer focuses on basing human actions upon the interpretation of meaning. The best example of this "root image" can be found in Royce's discussion of the wayward traveler who must interpret the meaning of a signpost that indicates where to go next. After the interpreted meaning is derived, the wayward traveler must choose which direction to go next. The concept of choosing a course of action based upon Royce's interpretive process plays a major role in his philosophy.

The final "root image" deals with the notion of "joint action" or the idea that there are larger societal-level actions. The only example of this image that can be found in Royce's works is his discussion of the concept, "community of interpretation." Royce's ideas on the process of interpretation level do not clearly correspond with Blumer's concepts of joint action at the individual or societal level.

In sum, based upon Blumer's synthesis and "root images" of symbolic interactionism in comparison with the later academic writings of Royce, Royce most definitely a made contribution to early symbolic interactionism. Royce's contributions can be broken down into several main points: (1) Royce's philosophy on the process of interpretation fits with Blumer's initial three major premises of symbolic interactionism; (2) with the exception of the direct mentioning of societal-level interactions and a formal discussion on "joint action," the philosophy presented by Royce in his later academic works correlate with the six "root images" described by Blumer; (3) while the synchronization of Royce's work with the "root images" presented by Blumer is not perfect, Royce was a contributor to and interacted with other major contributors to the development of symbolic interactionism. No one is arguing that Royce's philosophical work represents a stand-alone version of symbolic interactionism; (4) the contribution to symbolic interactionism that Royce made is neither minimal nor maximal, though in the grand scheme of symbolic interactionism, his philosophy occupies an important part in the history of the early and formative development of the theory. This is a point that is explored further in the final section.

Mead and Royce: Concluding Thoughts

The second major component for assessing Royce's contribution to symbolic interactionism is based on his link to the three major conceptual areas of (1) language and meaning, (2) deriving meaning, and (3.) The concept of the "generalized other" that are presented in Mead's book, *Mind, Self, and Society* (1934). Based on the conceptual areas listed above, a comparison of these three major areas in the later academic works of Royce answers the question of whether Royce made a significant contribution to classical symbolic interactionism. The answer is still, yes. This conclusion is evidenced by reinvestigating and reiterating the results from the chapter in which Mead and Royce were compared and contrasted. The crucial link between these social philosophers provides further evidence of Royce's contributions to the early development of symbolic interactionism.

In terms of the first conceptual component; language and meaning, there seems to be quite a bit of agreement between Mead and Royce. Mead viewed language, or signs, symbols, gestures, and significant symbols, as part of our everyday lives. People are continuously involved in the social intercourse of language whether it is part of an internal dialogue or dialogue with another person, such as a neighbor (external). While Royce did not define or mention language in any broad category, he presented the same fundamental elements of language: signs, symbols, and through his examples, gestures.

These language categories, though not as broad as Mead's conceptualizations, are still highly relevant to this research because while

Royce did not draw as many distinctions, he did accept that these different categories were always in full motion. Royce's lack of an overall definition of language in the broadest sense of the term does not suggest a dissimilarity but rather indicates that he was already in agreement with Mead's statement that "language is a part of social behavior" and that it contains "an indefinite number of signs or symbols which may serve the purpose of what we term 'language" (Mead 1992, 13–14).

Perhaps more important than the agreement of the importance of language in everyday human life is that both social philosophers viewed language as a process from which meaning could be derived. Mead saws language (signs, symbols, gestures, verbal gestures, non-verbal gestures, and significant symbols) as providing avenues from which people can derive and understand the meaning of the world around them. The illustrations of the signpost and how an individual can interpret and derive meaning from their facial expressions based upon their own information and the information of an individual's neighbor provide clear examples of Royce's acceptance of this point because language is the key component of both.

The second major component of Meadian thought that must be addressed is his conceptualization of deriving meaning. For Mead, the concept of meaning "arises and lies within the field of the relation between the gesture of a given human organism and the subsequent behavior of this organism as indicated to another human organism by that gesture. If that gesture indicates to another organism the subsequent behavior of the given organism, then it has meaning" (Mead 1992, 76).

Royce illustrates this same point in his example of how an individual can interpret their facial expressions based upon the reaction of their neighbor. In this example, a person is interpreting his or her own facial expressions based upon his or her neighbor's own facial reactions, all while trying to interpret and derive meaning from the conversation at hand. Both people in this example are trying to interpret and derive meaning from one another in a constant and simultaneous process. Both individuals are engaged in a conversation in and received.

This conversation between a person and his or her neighbor is similar to Mead's ideas on gestures because as the conversation between the two people in Royce's example takes place, there is an adjustment in the communication between both people. That is, the two people in the conversation are adjusting to the facial expressions and the meaning behind them as the actual conversation is taking place. Not only is there a simultaneous adjustment taking place, but both people are also deriving external and internal meaning from the conversational dialogue. The same can also be said of Royce's example of a signpost. Although there is no physical person engaged in a conversation, the sign represents a message with a dialogue that an individual must consider in the same manner as an individual's facial expressions.

The third and final major component of Mead's social philosophy is the "generalized other." Mead defines the concept of the "generalized other" as "the organized community or social group which gives to the individual his unity of self" (1992, 154). Not only does the social group give the self its unity, but also "the attitude of the generalized other is the attitude of the whole community" (Mead 1992, 154). Royce shares Mead's concept of the "generalized other" with his own idea called the "community of interpretation." This notion of a "community of interpretation" is similar to Mead's "generalized other" because both suggest that people are living within a shared community of understanding of the world around them.

They are both suggesting that this shared community of understanding has an effect on an individual's own experiences as they are influenced by the "generalized other" or the "community of interpretation." The only real disagreement is over the size or scale of the respective ideas of the "generalized other" and the "community of interpretation." Mead saw the concept of the "generalized other" as being on a large scale at the societal or cultural level, whereas Royce viewed his concept of the "community of interpretation" as more local or related to an individual's own immediate community, such as a hometown, city, or rural township. This disparity in the scale of concept visualization probably reflects the fact that Royce grew up in a world that was categorized more by towns and cities than states.

In sum, based upon the three major conceptual components that were compared and contrasted based on Mead's fundamental ideas on symbolic interactionism and Royce's later academic writings, there are most definitely conceptual similarities in that (1) both social philosophers agree that language is a social process that is an ongoing and important feature of human's everyday lives, (2) Mead and Royce are both in agreement that language is a vehicle for deriving meaning and understanding, (3) Royce and Mead share the idea that deriving meaning involves a sort of conversation in which people are adjusting one another's actions, and (4) the notion that there is a larger community of shared beliefs that can influence interpretive and deriving meaning processes is a shared belief.

These four crucial links between the basic ideas of Mead, as compared to the later academic works of Royce, illustrates—as it did in the case of Blumer's synthesized conceptualization of symbolic interactionism—that

Royce did make a significant contribution to early symbolic interactionist thought. The linkage of Royce's work to Mead, as stated before in the case of Blumer, does not represent an attempt to argue that Royce was a stand-alone contributor to symbolic interactionism. Instead, it shows that his ideas are linked to two of the major contributors to the early development of symbolic interactionist thought and that Royce predated Blumer and Mead. Royce's linkages between Blumer's and Mead's symbolic interactionist thoughts have far-reaching implications for the theory, perspective, and academic discipline known as symbolic interactionism. These implications are discussed below.

The Implications of Roycean Social Philosophy

The impact of adding the Royce's philosophy to the history and development of the theory of symbolic interactionism has several implications. The history of symbolic interactionist thought, the way it is presently constructed and understood, is missing an originator's contributions to the core concepts. Without Royce's ideas included in the development of symbolic interactionism, there is a piece missing from the historical timeline of symbolic interactionist thought.

Royce's philosophy provides researchers with a new and interesting perspective from which to utilize symbolic interactionism. The inclusion of Royce's writings into symbolic interactionist theory would contribute to the accuracy of the history of the ideas of this perspective. The addition of Royce's later academic writings to the main body of symbolic interactionist work will allow other researchers to further create links between his works and symbolic interactionism. The inclusion of Royce's work into symbolic interactionism will assist in creating a more complete version of the theory's perspective. This newfound understanding has the potential to open up new debates and resolve old ones. Royce's work has the potential to help other researchers through its use and application in inquiries undertaken by symbolic interactionists and other sociologists.

These implications have the potential to invoke change either in symbolic interactionism as a theoretical perspective or in terms of the historical timeline of symbolic interactionism. The changes that are possible can and will potentially alter the way symbolic interactionists and sociologists view the symbolic interactionist perspective as a whole. Because of the possibility of a large change within symbolic interactionist theory and the history of the theory itself, it can be definitively stated that through the evidence presented in this book that Royce's contribution to symbolic interactionism could have far-reaching implications and consequences beyond those already discussed.

REFERENCES

Blumer, Herbert. (1969). *Symbolic Interactionism: Perspective and Method.* California: University of California Press.

Brent, Joseph. (1998). *Charles Sanders Peirce: A Life.* Bloomington: Indiana University Press.

Mead, George Herbert. (1992). *Mind, Self, and Society.* Chicago: The University of Chicago Press.

Meltzer, Bernard N., Petras, John W., and Reynolds, Larry T. (1980). *Symbolic Interactionism: Genesis, varieties, and criticism.* Boston: Routledge & Keegan Paul.

Reynolds, Larry T. (1993). *Interactionism Exposition and Critique.* New York: General Hall Inc.

Royce, Josiah (1917). "Mind." *Encyclopaedia of Religion and Ethics.* New York: Charles Scribner's & Sons.

(1968). *The Philosophy of Josiah Royce.* Indiana: Hackett Publishing. Edited by John K. Roth

(2001). *Josiah Royce's Late Writings: A Collection of Unpublished and Scattered Works.* England: Thoemmes Press.

Stuhr, John J. (1987). *Classical American Philosophy: Essential Readings and Interpretive Essays.* New York: Oxford University Press.

INDEX

www.ingramcontent.com/pod-product-compliance
Lightning Source LLC
Chambersburg PA
CBHW071136280326
41935CB00010B/1252